JMeter Cookbook

70 insightful and practical recipes to help you successfully use Apache JMeter

Bayo Erinle

BIRMINGHAM - MUMBAI

JMeter Cookbook

First published: October 2014

Production reference: 1221014

Published by Packt Publishing Ltd.
Livery Place
35 Livery Street
Birmingham B3 2PB, UK.

ISBN 978-1-78398-828-0

www.packtpub.com

Cover image by Artie Ng (artherng@yahoo.com.au)

Credits

About the Author

Bayo Erinle is an author and senior software engineer with over 11 years of experience in designing, developing, testing, and architecting software. He has worked in various spectrums of the IT field, including government, commercial, finance, and health care. As a result, he has been involved in the planning, development, implementation, integration, and testing of numerous applications, including multi-tier, standalone, distributed, and Cloud-based applications. He is passionate about programming, performance, scalability, and all technology-related things. He is always intrigued by new technology and enjoys learning new things.

He currently resides in Maryland, USA, and when he is not hacking away at some new technology, he enjoys spending time with his wife, Nimota, and their three children, Mayowa, Durotimi, and Fisayo.

He has also authored *Performance Testing with JMeter 2.9, Packt Publishing*.

About the Reviewers

Yoann Ciabaud is an architect/developer with strong application architecture skills in Java/JEE, integration, and database environments. While mainly focused on application architecture, design, and development, Yoann also has extensive skills in infrastructure (networks, server, and operating systems) and the design, build, and configuration of development, test, and production environments.

He is currently working for an electronic financial transaction company called Monext in France. Including other project and line roles, Yoann has worked in large (more than 50) and small (sole team member) teams on complex distributed architectures based on a wide range of technologies.

> I would like to thank my lovely wife, who lets me spend time working on reviewing a book instead of having more family time together. I want to assure her, I will catch up soon.

Andrey Pokhilko is well known as the founder of JMeter-Plugins.org, an open source project that has been enhancing the JMeter user experience since 2009. While working on this project, he also led Load Testing Group at search giant Yandex (NASDAQ: YNDX), a position that provided him with invaluable experience in high-load performance testing. At Yandex, he developed the updated version of Yandex.Tank, an open source load testing tool.

Keen to apply his ideas to a wider range of load testing problems, Andrey left Yandex in 2014 to focus on building Loadosophia.org, a start-up that provides load test results analysis as a service.

Shantonu Sarker is a freelance software test automation engineer, currently working for oDesk/Elance/Staff.com. As a consultant, he works as a trainer in BITM (an institute of BASIS) and as an automation tester for several reputed companies in Bangladesh. He has his own start-up company named QualitySofts.

He has attended three professional training courses provided by BASIS (Bangladesh Association for Software and Information Services) on OOP, OOAD, and software design and architecture. He also has training in Agile development and testing (Kanban and Scrum) and security testing. He is also learning to speak Japanese and has passed the JLPT-L4 exam.

He has previously reviewed *Performance Testing with JMeter 2.9, Packt Publishing*.

I would like to thank my Guru, Mahajatok. Without his guidance, I would not be what I am today.

Federico Diaz Valpuesta is a Linux systems administrator currently living in Seville, Spain. He has extensive experience in the administration of local area networks and Linux servers.

He has been using Linux since 1999, starting with RedHat 7.2, and currently uses Debian. He has learned to use all the various "flavors" of Linux when he needs to solve a problem, so he usually installs Debian for web servers, CentOS for clustering, and Zentyal for small LANs, user management, and file/printer sharing.

Right now, he is working as a freelance web developer, deploying web apps in AWS, DigitalOcean, and Hetzner. He lends a hand in virtualization and helps everyone who wants to get started with Linux.

In addition to trying new things on his computer for long hours, he also likes mountain biking and watching TV. You can follow his activities on his blog or Twitter.

Žmicier Žaleźničenka holds a Master of Science degree in Computer Science from Delft University of Technology, the Netherlands. He is currently working as a software developer at TomTom in Amsterdam. His areas of interest include search engines, application monitoring software, and performance optimization of large-scale web applications. He has worked closely with JMeter, both during his studies and day-to-day development activities.

I'd like to thank Packt Publishing for giving me the opportunity to edit this publication.

www.PacktPub.com

Support files, eBooks, discount offers, and more

You might want to visit www.PacktPub.com for support files and downloads related to your book.

Did you know that Packt offers eBook versions of every book published, with PDF and ePub files available? You can upgrade to the eBook version at www.PacktPub.com and as a print book customer, you are entitled to a discount on the eBook copy. Get in touch with us at service@packtpub.com for more details.

At www.PacktPub.com, you can also read a collection of free technical articles, sign up for a range of free newsletters and receive exclusive discounts and offers on Packt books and eBooks.

http://PacktLib.PacktPub.com

Do you need instant solutions to your IT questions? PacktLib is Packt's online digital book library. Here, you can access, read and search across Packt's entire library of books.

Why Subscribe?

- ▶ Fully searchable across every book published by Packt
- ▶ Copy and paste, print and bookmark content
- ▶ On demand and accessible via web browser

Free Access for Packt account holders

If you have an account with Packt at www.PacktPub.com, you can use this to access PacktLib today and view nine entirely free books. Simply use your login credentials for immediate access.

Table of Contents

Preface

In today's ever-growing IT sector, users are growing increasingly impatient when faced with slow and unresponsive applications. Slow page load times and sluggish services could mean unsatisfactory customer experiences leading to fewer customer visits, which in the end translates to smaller profit margins for businesses. As such, it becomes increasingly important to a business's success to have fast, reliable, and responsive systems that give users a superb experience, foster growth, and increase revenue.

Performance testing is a type of testing intended to determine the responsiveness, reliability, throughput, interoperability, and scalability of a system and/or application under a given workload. It is critical and essential to the success of any software product launch and its maintenance. It also plays an integral part in scaling an application out to support a wider user base.

Apache JMeter is a free, open source, cross-platform performance testing tool that has been around since the late 90s. It is mature, robust, portable, and highly extensible. It has a large user base and offers lots of plugins to aid testing.

This book is a practical, hands-on guide that focuses on how to leverage Apache JMeter to meet your testing needs. With over 50 practical and carefully selected recipes, it will guide you through building robust and maintainable test scripts, Cloud testing, developing custom JMeter plugins, integrating JMeter into continuous delivery workflows, and much more. You will find a lot of useful knowledge here to apply to your current or future testing engagements. Whether you are a developer or tester, this book is sure to have an impact on you and provide you with valuable knowledge to help you achieve success in your future testing endeavors.

What this book covers

Chapter 1, JMeter Fundamentals, covers fundamental and intermediate skills to help you use JMeter efficiently.

Chapter 2, Handling Responses, details how to handle various server and application responses.

Chapter 3, Building Robust Test Plans with Controllers, covers five useful and often encountered JMeter controllers and how to apply them to your use cases.

Chapter 4, Testing Services, details how to test web services and supporting application resources with JMeter.

Chapter 5, Diving into Distributed Testing, takes an in-depth look at leveraging the Cloud for performance testing. We cover three Cloud providers and see how to roll our own when the need arises.

Chapter 6, Extending JMeter, covers how to extend JMeter with plugins. We also detail how to write your own JMeter plugin.

Chapter 7, Building, Debugging, and Analyzing the Results of Test Plans, discusses some useful components in JMeter and how to leverage them, as well as how to build realistic, robust, and maintainable scripts.

Chapter 8, Beyond the Basics, covers integrating JMeter into continuous delivery workflows, scaling JMeter, and many other advanced tips and pointers.

Appendix, Installing the Supporting Software Needed for This Book, covers how to install the supporting software and how to proceed with the recipes in the chapters.

What you need for this book

To follow along with the examples in this book, you will need the following:

- A computer with an Internet connection
- Apache JMeter: `http://jmeter.apache.org/`
- Java Runtime Environment (JRE) or Java Development Kit (JDK): `http://www.oracle.com/technetwork/java/javase/downloads/index.html`

In addition, for some recipes in *Chapter 1, JMeter Fundamentals*, you will need the following:

- Google Chrome Browser: `https://www.google.com/chrome/browser/`
- Apache Maven: `http://maven.apache.org/`
- YourKit Java Profiler: `http://www.yourkit.com/` (this is commercial ware, but the free trial will do to follow along with the recipe)
- A Heroku account: `http://www.heroku.com`
- Apache Tomcat: `http://tomcat.apache.org/download-70.cgi`

For *Chapter 5*, *Diving into Distributed Testing*, you will need the following:

- ▸ Vagrant: `http://www.vagrantup.com/`
- ▸ An AWS account: `http://aws.amazon.com/`
- ▸ A Flood.IO account: `https://flood.io/`
- ▸ A BlazeMeter account: `http://blazemeter.com`

For *Chapter 8*, *Beyond the Basics*, any free Java IDE will do. This includes the following:

- ▸ IntelliJ Community Edition: `http://www.jetbrains.com/idea/download/`
- ▸ Eclipse: `https://www.eclipse.org/downloads/`

The book contains pointers and additional helpful links to set all these up.

Who this book is for

This book is targeted primarily at developers and testers. Developers who have always been intrigued by performance testing and want to get in on the action will find it extremely useful, and will gain essential skills as they walk through the practical recipes in the book.

Testers will also benefit from this book since it will guide them through solving practical, real-world challenges when testing modern web applications, giving them ample knowledge to aid them in becoming better testers. Additionally, they will be exposed to certain helpful testing tools that will come in handy at some point in their testing careers.

Conventions

In this book, you will find a number of styles of text that distinguish between different kinds of information. Here are some examples of these styles and an explanation of their meaning.

Code words in text, database table names, folder names, filenames, file extensions, pathnames, dummy URLs, user input, and Twitter handles are shown as follows: "Open the `add_cookie_manager.jmx` test script."

A block of code is set as follows:

```
JMeterVariables:
JMeterThread.last_sample_ok=true
JMeterThread.pack=org.apache.jmeter.threads.SamplePackage@2ae97e14
START.HMS=053854
START.MS=1396517934834
START.YMD=20140403
TESTSTART.MS=1396702498383
speed=7.7
```

```
speed_g=1
speed_g0="speed":7.7
speed_g1=7.7
sunrise=1396694648
sunrise_g=1
sunrise_g0="sunrise":1396694648
sunrise_g1=1396694648
sunset=1396740883
sunset_g=1
sunset_g0="sunset":1396740883
sunset_g1=1396740883
```

When we wish to draw your attention to a particular part of a code block, the relevant lines or items are set in bold:

```
<body>
Posted by
<a href='/login'>login</a>
<a href='/register'>register</a>
```

Any command-line input or output is written as follows:

```
Adding newrelic:stark on frozen-headland-2987... done, v7 (free)

Use `heroku addons:docs newrelic` to view documentation.
```

New terms and **important words** are shown in bold. Words that you see on the screen, in menus or dialog boxes for example, appear in the text like this: "Press the **Record** button."

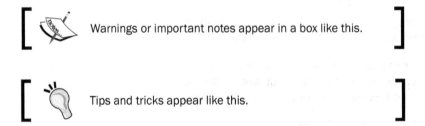

Warnings or important notes appear in a box like this.

Tips and tricks appear like this.

Reader feedback

Feedback from our readers is always welcome. Let us know what you think about this book—what you liked or may have disliked. Reader feedback is important for us to develop titles that you really get the most out of.

To send us general feedback, simply send an e-mail to feedback@packtpub.com, and mention the book title via the subject of your message. If there is a topic that you have expertise in and you are interested in either writing or contributing to a book, see our author guide on www.packtpub.com/authors.

Customer support

Now that you are the proud owner of a Packt book, we have a number of things to help you to get the most from your purchase.

Downloading the example code

You can download the example code files for all Packt books you have purchased from your account at http://www.packtpub.com. If you purchased this book elsewhere, you can visit http://www.packtpub.com/support and register to have the files e-mailed directly to you.

Errata

Although we have taken every care to ensure the accuracy of our content, mistakes do happen. If you find a mistake in one of our books—maybe a mistake in the text or the code—we would be grateful if you would report this to us. By doing so, you can save other readers from frustration and help us improve subsequent versions of this book. If you find any errata, please report them by visiting http://www.packtpub.com/submit-errata, selecting your book, clicking on the **errata submission form** link, and entering the details of your errata. Once your errata are verified, your submission will be accepted and the errata will be uploaded on our website, or added to any list of existing errata, under the Errata section of that title. Any existing errata can be viewed by selecting your title from http://www.packtpub.com/support.

Piracy

Piracy of copyright material on the Internet is an ongoing problem across all media. At Packt, we take the protection of our copyright and licenses very seriously. If you come across any illegal copies of our works, in any form, on the Internet, please provide us with the location address or website name immediately so that we can pursue a remedy.

Please contact us at copyright@packtpub.com with a link to the suspected pirated material.

We appreciate your help in protecting our authors, and our ability to bring you valuable content.

Questions

You can contact us at questions@packtpub.com if you are having a problem with any aspect of the book, and we will do our best to address it.

1

JMeter Fundamentals

In this chapter, we will cover the following recipes:

- ▸ Executing a test script
- ▸ Recording a script via HTTP(S) Test Script Recorder
- ▸ Recording scripts via the Chrome browser extension
- ▸ Converting HTTP web archives (HAR) to JMeter test plans
- ▸ Viewing and analyzing test results
- ▸ Feeding data into a script
- ▸ Using timers
- ▸ Managing HTTP user sessions
- ▸ Testing Single Page Applications (SPAs)
- ▸ Testing AJAX-centric applications

Introduction

In this chapter, you will learn the fundamentals and intermediate skills that will help you work better with JMeter. Tasks such as executing or recording scripts are routine and you can be almost certain that you will need to perform them, sometimes on a daily basis. Also, we will learn how to view and analyze the results of test executions, feed data into test scripts, and make test scripts mimic user behavior with the aid of timers. In later recipes, we dive into dealing with handling authentication, authorization, and testing today's new breed of applications with JMeter.

Executing a test script

Sometimes, the test scripts to execute have already been recorded and handed over to you to run. In this recipe, we will show you just how to go about executing a script that was prerecorded.

How to do it...

To execute a test script, perform the following steps:

1. Open the command line prompt.

2. Change to the directory of your JMeter install. We'll refer to this as JMETER_HOME.

    Refer to *Appendix* for JMeter installation instructions.

3. Change JMETER_HOME to the bin directory.

4. To launch the JMeter GUI on Windows, type in jmeter.bat. Alternatively, for Unix/Mac OS, type in ./jmeter.

5. Navigate to **File | Open**.

    Alternative key binding: Mac OS (*Command + O*), Windows (*Ctrl + O*).

6. Navigate to the script you want to execute. For example, ch1/getting_started.jmx provided with the sample code.

7. Press the green start icon at the top.

    Alternative key binding: Mac OS (*Command + R*), Windows (*Ctrl + R*).

8. View the results from one of the added listeners. If you are using getting_started.jmx from step 6, click on the **View Results Tree** listener as shown in the following screenshot:

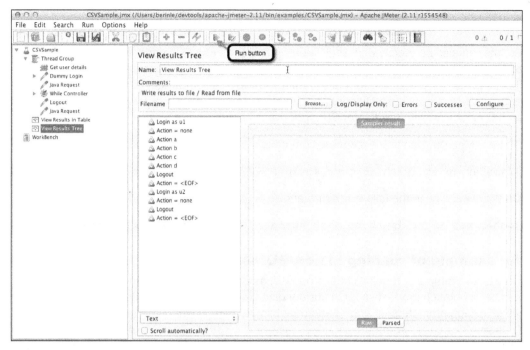

Executing a test script

How it works...

Test scripts are a series of prerecorded requests issued against an application. They are captured interactions of a user's actions with the application. These include visiting a URL, navigating around several pages, logging in, and so on. JMeter, like most test tools, has the ability to record and replay back test scripts. JMeter test scripts are stored in the XML (extendable markup language) format with the `.jmx` extension. Curious users can open the test script in a text editor of their choice (for example, Sublime Text, Notepad, and so on) and view exactly what it is doing, though, it is much more clear to understand what a script does by looking at it in JMeter's GUI.

After executing the test, results are reported through any configured listeners. A script can have one or several listeners attached to it (see recipes in *Chapter 7, Building, Debugging, and Analyzing the Results of Test Plans*).

There's more...

Scripts can also be executed in what JMeter refers to as non-GUI mode, which is completely on the command line without launching the JMeter GUI. To do this, instead of executing `jmeter.bat` or JMeter, like we did in step 4, we'll use certain JMeter command-line arguments to specify the test script and the resulting output file, which we can then go back and view with the JMeter GUI after the tests are executed.

On Unix/Mac OS, type in the following command:

```
./jmeter -n -t [path to test script] -l [path to results files]
```

On Windows, type in the following command:

```
jmeter.bat -n -t [path to test script] -l [path to results files]
```

An example of running in non-GUI mode

Here is an example of running code in non-GUI mode: This is how we executed the google_simulation.jmx test script in our bundled sampled in non-GUI mode. As you can see, we supplied parameters –n and –t and the absolute path to where our script is located (`/Users/berinle/workspace/jmeter-cookbook/ch1/google_simulation.jmx`) followed by the path to the results file (`/Users/berinle/workspace/jmeter-cookbook/ch1/google_simulation_result.csv`).

```
./jmeter -n -t /Users/berinle/workspace/jmeter-cookbook/ch1/google_
simulation.jmx -l /Users/berinle/workspace/jmeter-cookbook/ch1/
google_simulation_result.csv
```

Created the tree successfully using `/Users/berinle/workspace/jmeter-cookbook/ch1/google_simulation.jmx`.

Starting the test @ `Tue Feb 25 05:07:45 EST 2014 (1393322865378)`

Waiting for possible shutdown message on port `4445`.

Tidying up ...   @ Tue Feb 25 05:08:46 EST 2014 (1393322926156)

... end of run

Downloading the example code

You can download the example code files for all Packt books you have purchased from your account at `http://www.packtpub.com`. If you purchased this book elsewhere, you can visit `http://www.packtpub.com/support` and register to have the files e-mailed directly to you.

To view the results after the test has been executed, open up the JMeter GUI, create a new test plan, and add a listener to it by navigating to **Test plan | Add | Listener | Aggregate Report**. Click on the **Browse...** button to navigate to the location of the results file and open it. This is demonstrated in the following screenshot:

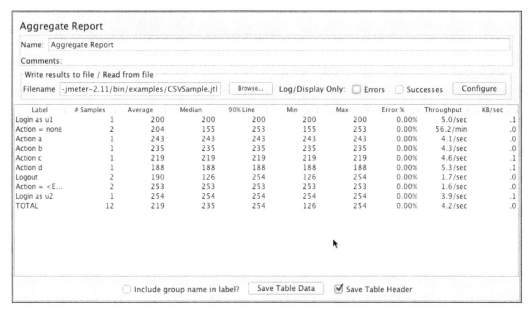

Viewing the results of a test run

There are several reasons why you might want to execute a test in non-GUI mode. Some of the reasons include:

- ▸ Running on a Unix machine with no GUI layer (that is, the JMeter GUI does not even open up)
- ▸ Running a distributed test
- ▸ Performance reasons of the JMeter GUI, which can sometimes be resource intensive; running in non-GUI mode alleviates this issue

Recording a script via HTTP(S) Test Script Recorder

Recording scripts is where you will spend most of your time. It is often the first step to develop test plans for applications. Though you can develop test plans manually by building them from within the JMeter GUI, or generating them via some domain-specific language (DSL), recording scripts by JMeter's HTTP(S) Test Script Recorder is one of the available options you have when building your test plans.

How to do it...

In this recipe, we cover how to record test scripts with HTTP(S) Test Script Recorder. Perform the following steps:

1. Start JMeter. Perform the following steps:

    ❑   Open the command-line prompt

    ❑   Change to the directory of your JMeter install (JMETER_HOME)

    ❑   Change to the `bin` directory

    ❑   Execute the following command:

    For Windows, type the following command:

    jmeter.bat

    For Mac OS/Unix, type the following command:

    ./jmeter

2. Once the GUI is opened, click on the **Templates...** button (the icon that appears immediately to the right of the new test plan icon) on the toolbar.

    [Templates were added in JMeter 2.10, so don't expect to see them in versions prior to that.]

3. In the drop-down menu of the **Select Template** box, choose **Recording** and click on the **Create** button.

4. Click on the **HTTP(S) Test Script Recorder** element (under **WorkBench**) and change **Port** (under **Global Settings**) from 8888 to 7000.

    ❑   You can use a different port if you want to. What is important to choose is a port that is not currently used by an existing process on the machine. The default is 8888.

5. Leave the rest of the components with the default set values.

6. The template does an excellent job and is configured with sensible defaults. The defaults provide the following:

    ❑ Target the recorded actions to **Recording Controller** added by the template.

    ❑ Group a series of requests that constitute a page load. We will see more on this topic later.

    ❑ Instruct the script recorder to bypass recording requests of a series of elements that are not relevant to test execution. These include JavaScript files, style sheets, and images.

    ❑ Add the often-used components, including user-defined variables, HTTP Request Defaults, and HTTP Cookie Manager, to the test plan.

    ❑ Add **Thread Group** and **Recording Controller** to the test plan.

    ❑ Add a **View Results Tree** listener to view results of the test plan.

7. Click on the **Start** button at the bottom of the **HTTP(S) Test Script Recorder** component.

With these settings, the test script recorder server will start on the port `7000`, monitor all requests going through that port, and record them to a test plan using the default recording controller. For details, see the following screenshot:

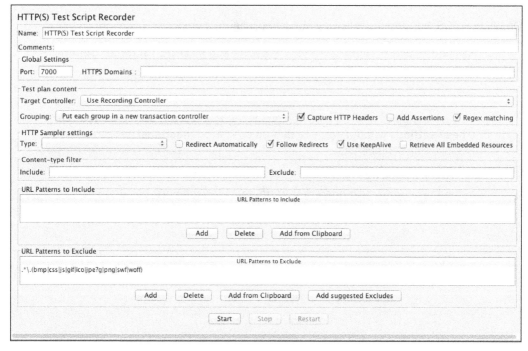

HTTP(S) Test Script Recorder configuration

How it works...

These steps instruct JMeter to act as an HTTP proxy and listen for incoming and outgoing requests from your browser to the Internet on the assigned port, in our case `7000`.

We now need to configure the browser to use the proxy server we just configured and redirect requests to the assigned port. There are several ways to do that, but we will focus here on the two most common ways.

There's more...

Modern browsers have a vibrant and active plugin ecosystem that allows you to extend the capabilities of your browser with an added plugin. **FoxyProxy** is one such plugin (`http://getfoxyproxy.org/`). It is a neat add-on for a browser that allows you to set up various proxy settings and toggle between them on the fly, without having to mess around with system settings on the machine. It really makes the work hassle free. Thankfully, FoxyProxy has a plugin for all major browsers including Google Chrome, Firefox, and Internet Explorer. If you are using any of those, you are lucky; head over and grab it!

Changing the machine system settings

The other common way to configure the browser is to change the system settings. The following are the details on how to configure Windows and Mac OS.

On Windows OS, perform the following steps to configure a proxy:

1. Navigate to **Start | Control Panel | Network and Internet | Internet Options**.
2. In the **Internet Options** dialog box, click on the **Connections** tab.
3. Click on the **LAN Settings** button.
4. To enable the use of a proxy server, check the **Use a proxy server for your LAN (These settings will not apply to dial-up or VPN connections)** box as shown in the following screenshot.
5. In the proxy **Address** box, enter `localhost` in the IP address.
6. In the **Port** number text box, enter `7000` (to match the port you set up for your JMeter proxy earlier).

7. If you want to bypass the proxy server for the local IP addresses, select the **Bypass proxy server for local addresses** checkbox.

8. Click on **OK** to complete the proxy configuration process. This is shown in the following screenshot:

Manually setting a proxy on Windows 7

On Mac OS, perform the following steps to configure a proxy:

1. Navigate to **System Preference | Network | Advanced...**.

2. Go to the **Proxies** tab.

3. Check **Web Proxy (HTTP)**.

4. Under **Web Proxy Server**, enter `localhost`.

5. For port, enter `7000` (to match the port you set up for your JMeter HTTP proxy earlier).

6. Do the same for **Secure Web Proxy (HTTPS)**.

7. Click on **OK**, as shown in the following screenshot:

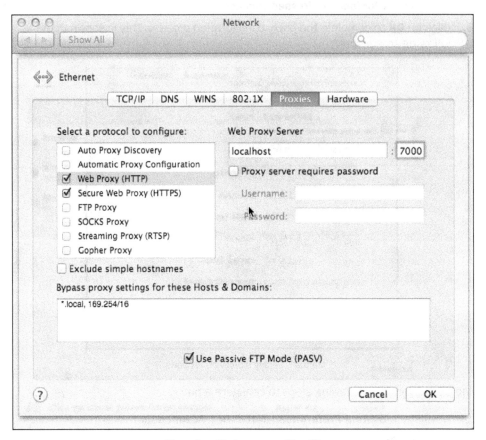

Manually setting a proxy on Mac OS

For all other systems, consult the related operating system documentation.

With both JMeter's HTTP(S) Test Script Recorder and browser configured to use it, we are now ready to record a test. Perform the following steps:

1. Point your browser to a website of your choice.

2. Navigate to a few links.

3. Notice that all user actions are being captured under the **Thread Group** component in the JMeter GUI.

4. Stop the recording by stopping HTTP(S) Test Script Recorder.

The HTTP(S) Test Script Recorder server is set up to listen to requests on a particular port and then set the browser or system to redirect all requests to the assigned port. This allows us to capture the user actions as they interact with web applications, allowing us to replay their actions like we did in the *Executing a test script* recipe.

See also

- The *Recording scripts via the Chrome browser extension* recipe in *Chapter 8, Beyond the Basics*
- The *Writing Test scripts through Ruby DSL* recipe
- The *Converting HTTP web archives (HAR) to JMeter test plan* recipe

Recording scripts via the Chrome browser extension

Recording test scripts is one you will be doing quite often. There are many alternatives to how we can record test scripts in JMeter.

How to do it...

In this recipe, we show you how to record test scripts with just a browser add-on installed on the Google Chrome browser. Perform the following steps:

1. Install the Google Chrome browser if it's not already installed on your machine.

 You can download it from `https://www.google.com/intl/en/chrome/browser/`.

2. Open the Chrome Web Store.
3. Search for `blazemeter` on the web store.
4. Install the BlazeMeter browser extension by clicking on the **Free** button.

 Once installed, a new BlazeMeter icon will be placed in the top-right corner of your browser toolbar.

5. Click on the newly added BlazeMeter extension button in the top-right corner of your browser toolbar.
6. Press the **Record** button.
7. Point your browser to a website of your choice.
8. Navigate through the website as you will normally do as a user.
9. After the previous step, stop the recording and click on the export to jmx button (**.jmx**). This will download a copy of your script to your local machine.
10. Open the exported test script in JMeter.

11. Add **View Results in Tree Listener** to the test plan (**Test plan | Add | Listener | View Results in Tree Listener**).

12. Run the exported test script with JMeter.

13. View the results.

Exporting your recorded test plan requires a free account with BlazeMeter for you to be logged in.

Installing the BlazeMeter Chrome extension

The BlazeMeter Chrome extension should look similar to what is shown in the preceding screenshot. Using this extension, additional properties can be configured in the **Advance** section of the extension. The following is a screenshot of the extension:

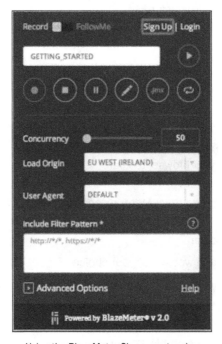

Using the BlazeMeter Chrome extension

How it works...

The browser extension captures the user interaction with the website in the JSON format as long as the recorder is on.

When the recording is stopped, no further user actions are captured. After the export button has been clicked on the JSON format is then converted to the XML format, which JMeter understands and can work with. The downloaded recorded script can then be edited and run within JMeter like any other script.

There's more...

The extension allows you to selectively capture requests by providing you with the ability to pause recording in between the user interactions. It also allows you to filter out unwanted traffic you might not be interested in capturing in your test scripts through the include filter pattern text area.

Furthermore, the **Advance** menu option allows you to gain more control over which requests are captured in your script, allowing you to capture only the top-level requests (default), disable browser cache (default), disable recording cookies (default), and edit the setting before proceeding to run.

Finally, as BlazeMeter (one of the many providers offering distributed testing in the Cloud) provides this extension, it offers additional features including the following:

▸ Allows you to run your scripts directly in the Cloud (see *Chapter 5, Diving into Distributed Testing*)

▸ Allows you to simulate thousands of users with ease (see *Chapter 5, Diving into Distributed Testing*)

Converting HTTP web archives (HAR) to JMeter test plans

Another alternative to recording test scripts in JMeter is converting the existing HTTP web archives directly into JMeter test scripts.

How to do it...

This recipe shows you how to generate a test script from captured HTTP web requests in your browser. Perform the following steps:

1. Install and launch the Google Chrome browser (if you don't already have it).
2. Open **Developer Tools** by navigating to **Tools | Developer Tools**.

Alternative key bindings: Mac OS (*Command + Shift + I*), Windows (*Ctrl + Shift + I*).

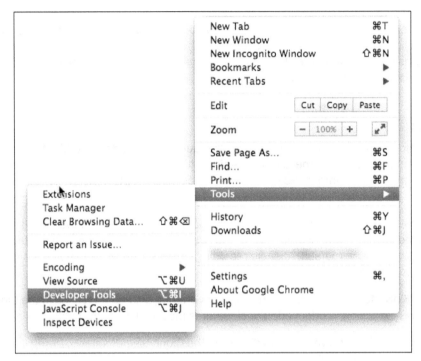

Opening Chrome Developer Tools

3. Click on the **Network** tab.

4. Make sure that the **Preserve log** checkbox is checked.

5. Browse the websites as you normally would.

6. Once you have finished browsing, open the developer tool window, right-click and select **Copy All as HAR**.

7. Point your browser to `https://flood.io/har2jmx`.

8. Copy the contents of the clipboard to the input box.

9. Click on the **Convert** button.

10. Launch the JMeter GUI.

11. Open and examine the downloaded test script.

12. Add **View Results in Tree Listener** to the test plan (**Test plan | Add | Listener | View Results in Tree Listener**).

13. Save and run the exported test script.

14. View the results.

Make sure that the **Preserve log** checkbox in the **Network** tab is checked to ensure all the user actions are captured, as illustrated in the following screenshot:

Preserve log checkbox in the Network tab

As shown in the following screenshot, while on the **Network** tab, right-click to see the **Copy All as HAR** option:

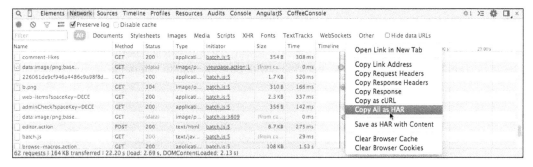

Copy All as HAR

How it works...

With the help of built-in browser tools and plugins, a browser is able to capture all interactions between a user and a web application into the **JSON (JavaScript Object Notation)** format known as the web archive (HAR). This resulting JSON object includes all the information about each request including HTTP headers, methods, query strings, and so on. Given the JSON object or a file with its content, the HAR to JMX converter can then read, parse, and construct JMeter elements for each user request, similar to what a JMeter HTTP proxy would have done.

There's more...

For command-line fans who do not wish to go through the Flood IO's website to do a conversion, there's a command-line tool that can be used to achieve the HAR TO JMX conversion. **Har2jmeter** located at `http://seitenbau.github.io/har2JMeter/` is a utility written in the Groovy language. It's still in its infancy, so you might encounter a few quirks here and there. While testing it, one thing we found out is that it currently didn't play well with secure connections (HTTPS). Also, it didn't group requests into logical controllers. We mention it here just to make you aware that it exists and such bugs will probably be fixed in the near future.

> For Firefox, the firebug plugin allows you the same capability to capture requests as HAR. Visit `http://www.ehow.com/how_8789702_create-har-files-using-firebug.html` to see how this can be accomplished.

Viewing and analyzing test results

When it comes to viewing your test results, JMeter comes with a vast number of components to aid this regard. Each component gives a different perspective into how to visualize your test results. Deciding which to use depends mostly on what kind of data you are interested in for a test run. Also, JMeter doesn't place a limit on how many of these listeners you can use on a test script, so it's not uncommon to see scripts with several results listeners.

How to do it...

In this recipe, we will cover three of the most popular built-in viewing components you will most likely need for your scripts. This is by no means an exhaustive list, so be sure to explore other viewing components. Perform the following steps:

1. Launch JMeter.
2. Open a previously recorded test script.
3. Add a **View Results Tree** listener by navigating to **Test plan | Add | Listener | View Results Tree**.
4. Add a **Aggregate Report** listener by navigating to **Test plan | Add | Listener | Aggregate Report**.
5. Add **View Results in table** by navigating to **Test plan | Add | Listener | View Results In Table**.
6. Start the test.
7. Examine the results on each of the added results listeners. The entire process is shown in the following screenshot:

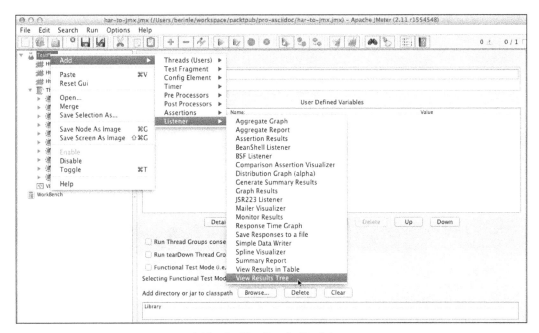

Adding the View Results Tree listener

The **View Results Tree** component is shown in the following screenshot:

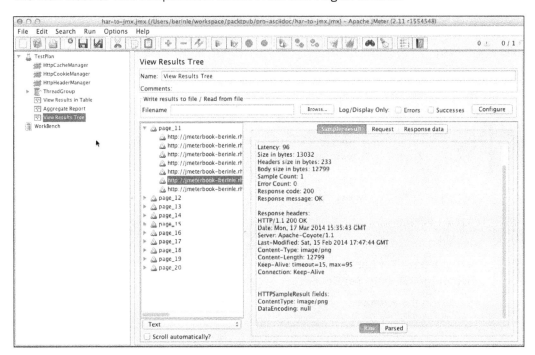

How it works...

Once added, the test results will be written in real time to these listeners as the test is going on. Each listener gives a different data representation of the test results. Depending on what you are interested in, you will use a different set of listeners.

There's more...

There are graph listeners that plot graphs in real time, helping you visualize your test results in a graphical way. Also, there are extensions to JMeter that provide even additional result listeners just in case you need more than the built-in listener components.

Feeding data into a script

More often than not, we will need to provide varying input datasets to our scripts to simulate realistic user interaction with an application. Most applications, for instance, need to be authenticated against to view certain restrictive areas of the application. The way to accomplish this is by supplying an input datafile to the test script. The file is normally in the form of **comma-separated values** (**CSV**).

How to do it...

This recipe shows you how to feed data into your script to handle such scenarios. Perform the following steps:

1. Download the book code samples from
   `http://www.packtpub.com/jmeter-cookbook/book`.

    Alternatively, you can clone the sample from the GitHub repository at
   `http://github.com/jmeter-cookbook/bundled-code`.

2. Extract the contents of the ZIP file.
3. Launch JMeter.
4. Open the `ch1_feed_me_data.jmx` script from the `scripts/ch1` directory.
5. Add **CSV Data Set Config** to the test plan by navigating to **Test Plan | Add | Config Element | CSV Data Set Config**. Let's configure it:
    1. In the **Filename** box, enter `input.txt`.
    2. Leave the rest of the entries blank.

6. Save and run the test. The execution of the script is shown in the following screenshot:

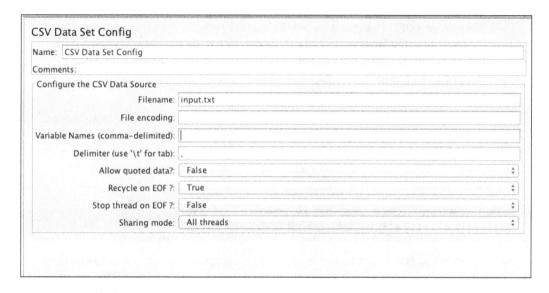

How it works...

Assuming you haven't changed the default sharing mode of the added CSV dataset configuration, with each iteration run of our test plan, a line of the `input.txt` file is consumed. The consumed values are then turned into JMeter variables named after the first line of our input datafile, which are `user` and `pass` in our case. The values are then used further down the execution chain to fill in the username and password to access our application. In this particular test plan, as we have more threads than the amount of input data, the input data is recycled once the end of the file is reached.

There's more...

In our example, we have just provided the name of the file to read the input feed from. If you examine the CSV dataset configuration element closely, you will notice that it has other properties that can be filled in. These include the following:

▶ **Variable Names**: Provide the comma-separated names of the variables. As we left this blank, the first line of our input script will be treated as the variable name.

▶ **Delimeter**: Change to this option if you want to use a different delimiter other than a comma. For instance, you can use tab spaces (`\t`) or the colon symbol (`:`) instead of commas.

- ▶ **Allow Quoted Data**: Set to **True**, if you would like to allow quoted data. For example, `'hello'` as opposed to `hello`.

- ▶ **Recycle on EOF**: In cases where you have more threads than the input data, this attribute specifies whether to allow the input data to be recycled. In such a case, the input feed will start from the beginning of the file once the data feed has run out.

- ▶ **Stop thread on EOF**: This option determines whether to kill the thread has been reached.

- ▶ **Sharing mode**: The default option is `All` meaning all threads; even those in a different thread group get to share the same data. The other options are **Current thread group** and **Current thread**, which specify that only the threads within a particular thread group and only a particular thread can retrieve data from the file, respectively.

Using timers

By default, when test scripts are recorded in JMeter, they contain no pauses between page requests. This is sometimes known as the **think time** in test scripts. In reality though, most users will frequently pause for a duration of time on every page before moving on to another page in the application. In JMeter, the ways to achieve these pauses are through timers. JMeter comes with a wealth of timers to achieve this purpose.

How to do it...

In this recipe, we will show you how to mimic realistic user behaviors using the JMeter timers.

1. Launch JMeter.
2. Open the `ch1_add_timers.jmx` test script located in the `scripts/ch1` directory.
3. Add **Gaussian Random Timer** by navigating to **Test plan | Add | Gaussian Random Timer**.
4. Change **Deviation (in milliseconds)** from `100` to `1000`.
5. Change **Constant Delay Offset (in milliseconds)** from `300` to `500`.
6. Save and execute the test script.

How it works...

With our configuration, each thread will pause for a duration of `0.5` to `1.5` seconds after each request before proceeding to the next request. This is because we applied the timer at the root level of the test plan. If we wanted to have pauses after each logical page rendering, we will add a timer at the transaction controller level. This option is mostly what you will go with as a single rendered web page often consists of multiple requests.

There's more...

There are many more timers that come bundled with JMeter even through additional plugins that serve different purposes. There are timers that simulate constant delay, constant throughput, random delay, and so much more. Depending on your use case and what you are trying to simulate, you will choose one or several of these.

Managing HTTP user sessions

Most websites have a means of authenticating users, thereby enabling them to gain access to protected data or content that only pertains to them. Also, it is very common for websites to give users different roles based on what the user will be doing. For instance, a user called `Joe` could be given admin privileges while `Susan` is only given user privileges. Whatever the case, JMeter has a way to maintain HTTP user sessions for your test scripts.

How to do it...

In this recipe, we will detail how to accomplish this with JMeter. Perform the following steps:

1. Launch JMeter.
2. Open the `add_cookie_manager.jmx` test script.
3. Run the test plan.
4. Notice the failed requests, even though the log in request succeeded:
    - The **Request immediately** option following the log in request is indicative of this. The **Request** tab shows no cookies were sent with the request. Refer to the following code:
      ```
      GET http://evening-citadel-2263.herokuapp.com/
       [no cookies]
      Request Headers:
      Connection: keep-alive
      Host: evening-citadel-2263.herokuapp.com
      User-Agent: Apache-HttpClient/4.2.6 (java 1.5)
      ```
    - Furthermore, our response assertions fail, as subsequent requests were not associated with the existing user, but were treated as new requests.
5. Clear the results (Mac OS: *Command + Shift + E* and Windows: *Ctrl + Shift + E*).
6. Add **HTTP Cookie Manager** to the test plan by navigating to **Test plan | Add | Config Element | HTTP Cookie Manager**.
7. Save and run the test plan.

8. Observe the results in the **View Results in Tree** listener and notice how all the requests now succeed:

   ❑ If you observe the request immediately following the log in request, you will notice that the cookie information is correctly sent with the request, thanks to the added HTTP Cookie Manager. You should see something similar to this:

```
GET http://evening-citadel-2263.herokuapp.com/
Cookie Data:
connect.sid=s%3AWN5ITZxWEKyzmmAB5sct7PjA.6UAJ36%2F9%2BWFQPjd
zA%2B7%2B1NL4%2Bf0HzC%2BOQI%2Bol0V0eJ0
Request Headers:
Connection: keep-alive
Host: evening-citadel-2263.herokuapp.com
User-Agent: Apache-HttpClient/4.2.6 (java 1.5)
```

How it works...

The HTTP Cookie Manager stores and sends cookies like a web browser does. The cookie of any request that contains one is automatically extracted and stored by the component to be used for all future requests from that particular thread. Each JMeter thread gets its own session just like in a regular web browser to prevent users' sessions from overlapping with each other.

There's more...

Apart from the automatically extracted cookies by the HTTP Cookie Manager component, JMeter provides a way to add user-defined cookie values to a test plan. Unlike their automatically extracted counter parts, once defined, all threads executing in the test plan will share these values.

Testing Single Page Applications (SPAs)

Single-page applications are the new wave of web applications being developed in today's technological industry. The benefits of developing such applications can't be overstated. They relieve the servers of enormous load and bring faster responsiveness to the end user. They are architected differently from traditional web applications, which make them slightly different to develop test scripts for.

How to do it...

In this recipe, we will work through creating a script for an SPA. Perform the following steps:

1. Launch JMeter.

2. Add **HTTP(S) Test Script Recorder** and set it up for recording (see the *Recording a script via JMeter HTTP proxy* recipe).

3. Click the **Add suggested Excludes** button.

4. Start the HTTP(S) Test Script Recorder.

5. Point your browser to `http://angular.github.io/peepcode-tunes/public/`.

6. Add the two available albums (on the right) to your playlist (on the left).

7. Randomly select a song to listen to.

8. Use the buttons on the player to jump to the next or previous song or pause them.

9. Stop the HTTP(S) Test Script Recorder.

10. Add a listener to your test plan.

11. Save and run the test plan.

How it works...

The actions of the user are tracked and recorded via the script recorder we set up in step 2. Like traditional web applications, we record all actions and exclude irrelevant static resources, such as images, JavaScript, and style sheets. Every call that makes a server call to backend services is also recorded as part of the test plan and is available for replay during test execution. At the end, we have a script that is almost identical to what we would get when recording a traditional web application.

There's more...

Most SPAs tend to be JavaScript-intensive. As JMeter isn't a web browser, JavaScripts embedded within a page or included from a separate file altogether won't be executed. With this in mind, it means JMeter can't be accurately used to measure page load times or browser DOM rendering. What it can do, however, is record any calls made to the server from your JavaScript files and play those back when the test is re-executed.

Such calls have an impact on the servers and are critical to measure to know how slow or fast a user's experience will be when the application is under considerable load.

Testing AJAX-centric applications

In today's stack of web applications, it is almost unthinkable to build an application without some dynamic content being retrieved from a backend service. Most of the time, these applications tend to lean towards partial page fresh. That is, only the needed sections of a rendered page are refreshed as opposed to the whole page loading its entire content again. This leads to more responsive pages, which improves the overall experience of the user.

How to do it...

In this recipe, we will walk through how you can test such applications using JMeter. Perform the following steps:

1. Launch JMeter.

2. Add **HTTP(S) Test Script Recorder** and set it up for recording (see the *Recording a script via JMeter HTTP proxy* recipe).

3. Click the **Add suggested Excludes** button.

4. Start the HTTP(S) Test Script Recorder.

5. Point your browser to `https://maps.google.com`.

6. Perform a couple of searches in the provided search box (for example, pizza, restaurants, hotels, and so on).

7. Click on a few of the returned results.

8. Repeat steps 6 and 7 two more times.

9. Stop the HTTP(S) Test Script Recorder.

10. Add a listener to your test plan.

11. Save and run the test plan.

How it works...

The actions of the user are tracked and recorded via the script recorder we set up in step 2. Like traditional web applications, we record all actions and exclude irrelevant static resources, such as images, JavaScript, and style sheets. Calls that trigger backend server calls are trapped and are available for replay later. At the end, we have a script that is almost identical to what we would get when recording a traditional web application.

There's more...

AJAX-centric applications tend to involve a lot of asynchronous server requests made from within the client (frontend). These calls are normally made from embedded script tags within a view technology, for example, HTML, **Java Server Pages** (**JSP**), **Groovy Server Pages** (**GSP**), or from an included JavaScript file in the page. As such, JMeter records all such server requests and they can be played back at the time of running our test plans. This allows us to simulate the intended load on our servers, as though the application was the one making the AJAX calls.

2
Handling Responses

In this chapter, we will cover the following recipes:

- ▶ Using Regular Expression Extractor
- ▶ Using Regular Expression Tester
- ▶ Using CSS/jQuery Extractor
- ▶ Using XPath Extractor
- ▶ Dealing with file downloads
- ▶ Handling XML responses
- ▶ Handling JSON responses
- ▶ Handling HTML responses
- ▶ Using Response Assertion
- ▶ Using Duration Assertion
- ▶ Uploading files with your scripts

Introduction

When testing applications, it is important to know how to handle the responses from the several requests that constitute the test script. In this chapter, we will tackle how to deal with various server responses for applications under test. These include handling XML, JSON, and HTML responses. It's even more important to know how to extract information contained in those responses, as you might need them to feed data dynamically to your script down the execution chain. Preprocessors and postprocessors, as their names imply, are applied before and after samplers respectively to extract information from server responses, which can then be stored and used later down the execution chain. In the later recipes, we cover how to handle file uploads with JMeter and assert the correctness of such responses.

Using Regular Expression Extractor

JMeter comes bundled with a Regular Expression Extractor component that gives you fine-grained control over what to extract from a server response using regular expression syntax. Readers familiar with regular expression syntax will feel right at home, but don't worry if you haven't used regular expressions before. Regular expressions are special characters that match portions of a field based on a set of rules defined by a regular expression pattern. More information about regular expressions can be found on `http://en.wikipedia.org/wiki/Regular_expression` or by searching on the Internet.

How to do it...

In this recipe, we will cover how to use the Regular Expression Extractor component in JMeter to extract server responses to make our test script dynamic in nature. Perform the following steps:

1. Launch JMeter.

2. Open the `ch2_regex.jmx` test script located in the `scripts/ch2` directory.

3. Run the script.

4. Observe the errors in the **View Results Tree** listener. Notice the response code is `403`, indicating a forbidden request. This is shown in the following code:

   ```
   Headers size in bytes: 319
   Body size in bytes: 1081
   Sample Count: 1
   Error Count: 1
   Response code: 403
   Response message: Forbidden

   Response headers:
   HTTP/1.1 403 Forbidden
   Content-Type: application/json
   Date: Wed, 09 Apr 2014 09:52:40 GMT
   Set-Cookie: connect.sess=s%3Aj%3A%7B%22_csrf%22%3A%22scyJ6YXNZ4rjd
   AXXy8DkD3Yy%22%7D.eygkOhdJO%2B%2BkLd5%2FWcz0wZUFjpnyYtOeC18%2BrUx7
   hv8; Path=/; HttpOnly
   ```

5. Add **Regular Expression Extractor** to the request labeled **add_regex_here** by navigating to **add_regex_here | Add | Post Processors | Regular Expression Extractor**.

6. Fill in the values as follows:

```
Response Field to check: Headers
    Reference Name: token
    Regular Expression: XSRF-TOKEN=(.+);
    Template: $1$
    Match No. (0 for Random): 0
    Default Value: NOT_FOUND
```

7. Save and re-run the script.

8. Observe that the errors are now gone and the post is successful. This is shown in the following screenshot:

How it works...

The test script is recorded for a site that uses **Cross-Site Request Forger** (**CSRF**) to prevent against malicious attacks that prey on user vulnerability. As such, a token is attached to each user's session that is then sent along with every request from that user. Each user gets their own unique token, and therefore, using the same token for two users flags an error on the server and the request is denied. That is exactly what happened in step 4.

In steps 5 and 6, we extracted the CSRF token with the aid of Regular Expression Extractor, and correctly sent the unique token for the rest of the requests for that user in the test script. Doing so allowed each request to be completed successfully.

There's more...

This is only one way Regular Expression Extractor can be used. There are several more cases where it could come to the rescue. These include the following:

- Extracting URL paths
- Extracting HTML responses
- Extracting XML responses
- Extracting JSON responses

You will find yourself using Regular Expression Extractor quite a lot in your testing scenarios.

> To get the most out of Regular Expression Extractor, read more on regular expressions. Understanding regular expressions is critical to defining the correct pattern matches in your test script.

Using Regular Expression Tester

When trying to extract parts of a server response through a regular matching expression, Regular Expression Tester is your best friend. This component allows you to test your regular expression patterns directly on the sampler response data. Without such a component, it will be daunting to nail down the exact regular expression to fulfill your matching needs. This component comes bundled as part of the **View Results Tree** listener.

How to do it...

In this recipe, we cover the use of Regular Expression Tester:

1. Launch JMeter.
2. Open the `ch2_regex_tester.jmx` test script located in the `scripts/ch2` directory.
3. Run the test plan.
4. Click on the **View Results Tree** listener.
5. In the bottom-left corner of the **View Results Tree** listener, select the **RegEx Tester** option.

6. In the **Regular expression** textbox, enter a regular expression to extract information from the server response. We can proceed in the following way:

   ❑ Let's say we wanted to extract the `xsrf` token; we will use the regular expression `'xsrf':'(\w+)'`

   ❑ To extract the search ID, we could use **searchId =\s+\"(\d+)\"**

   ❑ To extract the user region, we could use **region":\s+"(\w+)**, and so on

7. Once we have the right regular expression, we could then apply it to the HTTP sampler to correctly execute our test plan. This is shown in the following screenshot:

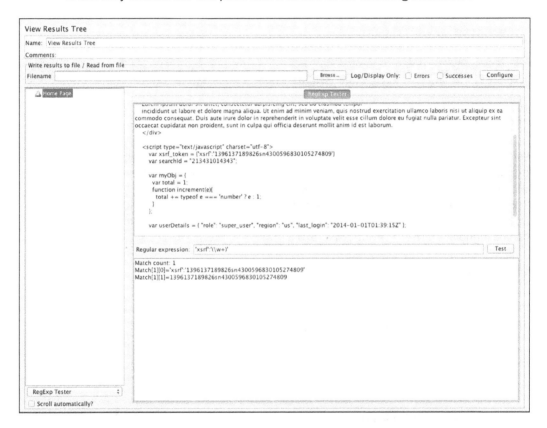

How it works...

Regular Expression Tester executes directly on the sampler response data since it is bundled as part of the results listener. As a result, we are able to refine our regular expression to our content without needing to re-execute our test script. This is a huge time saver and makes what could otherwise be a daunting task simple, in a sense.

There's more...

Regular expressions are extremely expressive and powerful. It is beyond the scope of this book to cover all the different syntax that could be used. For more information on regular expressions, some good starting resources are:

- ► http://jmeter.apache.org/usermanual/regular_expressions.html
- ► http://en.wikipedia.org/wiki/Regular_expression
- ► http://www.vogella.com/tutorials/JavaRegularExpressions/ article.html
- ► http://www.regexr.com/

Using CSS/jQuery Extractor

JMeter offers CSS/jQuery Extractor that allows you to extract server responses using a CSS/jQuery-like syntax. This component was introduced in JMeter 2.9 and is particularly helpful when dealing with HTML responses. CSS/jQuery-like syntax allows you to easily select HTML DOM elements that might otherwise have been difficult to write a regular expression for, for example, selecting a button with a `danger` class in the response (`button.danger`), selecting images matching a particular regular expression (`img[src~=(?i)\\.(png|jpeg|gif)]`), and so on. The default implementation of the CSS/jQuery implementation is JSoup (`http://jsoup.org`) and the API documentation for its selector can be found at `http://jsoup.org/apidocs/org/jsoup/select/Selector.html`.

How to do it...

In this recipe, we will cover how to use the CSS/jQuery Extractor component to extract information from server responses. Perform the following steps:

1. Launch JMeter.
2. Open the `ch2_css_jquery.jmx` test script located in the `scripts/ch2` directory.
3. Open the HTTP request labeled `add_css_jquery_here`.
4. Add **CSS/JQuery Expression Extractor** by navigating to **Request | Add | Post Processor | CSS/JQuery Extractor**.
5. Fill in the values as follows:

   ```
   Reference Name: post
   CSS/JQuery expression: div.entry p:matches(\w+)
   Attribute:
   Match No. (0 for Random): 0
   Default Value: NOT_FOUND
   ```

6. Save and run the script.

7. Open **Debug Sampler** and check whether the expression matches the intended query. This is shown in the following screenshot:

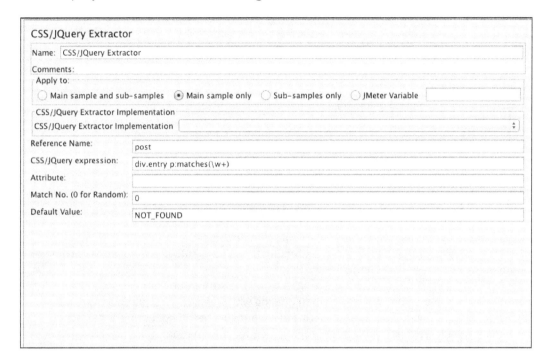

How it works...

As a postprocessor component, CSS/jQuery Extractor acts on requests within its scope and applies the specified CSS or jQuery expression, extracting all matches and storing them after what we specify in JMeter's session. This can then be referred to by other requests later in the execution chain.

In our case, we extracted all the div elements that matched a paragraph.

There's more...

Because of the flexibility provided by expression syntax, this component can't be fully covered within this book, but we encourage you to read more on CSS/jQuery syntax to fully harness the power of this component.

Some good starting resources are:

- ▶ `http://jsoup.org/apidocs/org/jsoup/select/Selector.html`
- ▶ `http://www.w3schools.com/cssref/css_selectors.asp`

Also, at the time of writing this, there is another implementation (`Lagarto`) syntax that is supported right out of the box by JMeter. Details can be found at `http://jodd.org/doc/lagarto/index.html`.

> Compared to Regular Expression Extractor, CSS/jQuery Extractor is resource-intensive as it does a complete HTML parse of the document to perform its work. In cases where Regular Expression Extractor can do the work, use that instead.

Using XPath Extractor

When it comes to dealing with XML or (X)HTML, JMeter comes bundled with an XPath Extractor component that allows you to extract matches from XML server responses using an XPath query language. For instance, extracting the title of a standard HTML structure can be accomplished using `html/head/title`, getting all the paragraphs can be accomplished using `body/p`, and so on. Moreover, when dealing with web services, particularly SOAP services, XMLs are used heavily as a means of exchange. This component is a perfect fit for handling such responses and extracting the needed information.

How to do it...

In this recipe, we will cover how to use XPath Extractor to handle XML server responses. Perform the following steps:

1. Launch JMeter.
2. Open the `ch2_xpath_extractor.jmx` test script located in the `scripts/ch2` directory.
3. Open the HTTP request labeled **add_xpath_extractor_here**.
4. Add **XPath Extractor** to it by navigating to **Request | Add | Post Processor | XPath Extractor**.
5. Fill in the values as follows:

   ```
   Reference Name: author
   XPath query: /bookstore/book/author[1]
   Default Value: NOT_FOUND
   ```

6. Save and run the script

7. Open **View Results Tree** and check whether the expression actually matches the intended query. This is shown in the following screenshot:

How it works...

As a postprocessor component, XPath Extractor acts on request within its scope and applies the specified XPath jQuery expression to it, extracting all matches and storing the match under an attribute named in **Reference Name**. This can then be referred to by other requests later in the execution chain.

In our case, we extracted all the first authors in the returned XML response from the server.

There's more...

Because of the flexibility provided by expression syntax, this component can't be fully covered within this book, but we encourage you to read more on the XPath query syntax to fully harness the power of this component.

A good starting resource is `http://www.w3schools.com/xpath/xpath_syntax.asp`.

Dealing with file downloads

It is not uncommon to come across scenarios where you need to simulate downloading a file or multiple files from an external server when recording your test scripts. JMeter provides the ability to record and play back file downloads.

How to do it...

In this recipe, we will cover how to use JMeter in a file download scenario. Perform the following steps:

1. Launch JMeter.

2. Add **Thread Group** to the new test plan by navigating to **Test Plan | Add | Threads (Users) | Thread Group**.

3. Add the **HTTP Request** sampler by navigating to **Thread Group | Add | Sampler | HTTP Request**.

4. Fill in its attributes in the following way:
   - **Server Name or IP**: docs.spring.io
   - **Method**: GET
   - **Path**: /spring-data/jpa/docs/1.5.x/reference/pdf/spring-data-jpa-reference.pdf

5. Add the **View Results Tree** listener to the test plan by navigating to **Test Plan | Add | Listener | View Results Tree**.

6. Add **Save Responses** to the file listener of your test script by navigating to **Test plan | Add | Listener | Save Responses to file**.

7. Fill in the following attributes:
   - **Filename prefix**: springdata_
   - **Variable Name**: manual

8. Save and run the test plan.

9. Observe the results in the **View Results Tree** listener. You should have an output similar to this:

```
Response too large to be displayed. Size: 224921 > Max:
204800, Start of message:
%PDF-1.4
%ª«¬
4 0 obj
<<
```

```
        /Title (Spring Data JPA - Reference Documentation)
        /Author (Oliver Gierke, Thomas Darimont, and Christoph Strobl)
        /Creator (DocBook XSL Stylesheets with Apache FOP)
        /Producer (Apache FOP Version 1.0)
        /CreationDate (D:20140313175008+01'00')
    >>
    endobj
        ...
```

Navigate to the `bin` directory of your JMeter install (`$JMETER_HOME/bin`) and you should see a PDF named `springdata_1.pdf` that has been downloaded there.

How it works...

We created a script that made a request to download a PDF file off an external server. We then added **Save Responses** to a file component of our test script. This component allows us to save the responses we get from a server to a file for later analysis or use. In this case, the server responded with a PDF file, which we then saved as a local file in the `bin` directory of our JMeter install directory. At the same time, we were able to verify the resources returned from the server by examining the **Response Data** tab in **View Results Tree**.

The name of the file is determined by the attributes we specified in step 7. Since we ran this once, there was no file already named `springdata_1.pdf` in the `bin` directory, and so one was created with that name. Subsequent runs will produce files named `springdata_x.pdf`, where `x` represents the number of runs.

The `prefix` filename can also be used to specify an alternative location to download the files to instead of cluttering up your `$JMETER_HOME/bin` directory. For example, you can specify `/tmp/springdata_` (or any valid directory path on your system) to have the files downloaded to that location instead.

There's more...

In our use case, we have chosen to use **Save Responses** to store our downloads in a file component. You would normally want to use this component when dealing with file downloads within your test plan, since it is able to download the contents of the resource and make it available to you locally. For example, we could go further by processing the downloaded file and uploading it to another server altogether through FTP, or consuming an uploading service at the targeted server.

Handling XML responses

Sometimes, the responses coming from the server are in XML format. Knowing how to handle such responses to extract the information needed by your scripts is an important aspect of building dynamic and robust scripts. Such scenarios might involve consuming web services or doing data manipulation to post to an external data source.

How to do it...

In this recipe, we will cover how to use JMeter to extract information from XML responses while consuming a freely available weather service. Perform the following steps:

1. Launch JMeter.

2. Add **Thread Group** to the new test plan by navigating to **Test Plan | Add | Threads (Users) | Thread Group**.

3. Add the **HTTP Request** sampler by navigating to **Thread Group | Add | Sampler | HTTP Request**.

4. Fill in its attributes in the following way:

   ❑ **Server Name or IP**: api.openweathermap.org

   ❑ **Method**: GET

   ❑ **Path**: /data/2.5/weather

5. Add the following request parameters to the request by clicking on the **Add** button:

Name	Value
q	London, UK
mode	XML

6. Add three XPath Extractors to **HTTP Request** by navigating to **HTTP Request | Add | Post Processors | XPath Extractor**.

7. Fill in the following details for the three XPath Extractors respectively:

Reference Name	XPath query	Default Value
sunrise	/current/city/sun/@rise	NOT_FOUND
sunset	/current/city/sun/@set	NOT_FOUND
wind	/current/wind/direction/@name	NOT_FOUND

8. Add the **View Results Tree** listener to the test plan by navigating to **Test Plan | Add | Listener | View Results Tree**.

9. Add **Debug Sampler** to the test plan by navigating to **Thread Group | Add | Sampler | Debug Sampler**.

10. Save and run the test plan.

11. Observe the results in the **View Results Tree** listener. You should have an output similar to this:

```
<current>
   <city id="2643743" name="London">
<coordlon="-0.13" lat="51.51"/>
      <country>GB</country>
      <sun rise="2014-04-04T05:27:38" set="2014-04-
04T18:39:07"/>
   </city>
   <temperature value="287.91" min="286.15" max="290.37"
unit="kelvin"/>
   <humidity value="36" unit="%"/>
   <pressure value="1009" unit="hPa"/>
   <wind>
     <speed value="2.57" name="Light breeze"/>
     <direction value="257" code="WSW" name="West-southwest"/>
   </wind>
   <clouds value="44" name="scattered clouds"/>
   <precipitation mode="no"/>
   <weather number="802" value="scattered clouds" icon="03d"/>
   <lastupdate value="2014-04-04T16:09:34"/>
</current>
```

12. Navigate to **Debug Sampler** and observe our XPath queries matched as expected. Refer to the following code:

```
JMeterVariables:
JMeterThread.last_sample_ok=true
JMeterThread.pack=org.apache.jmeter.threads.
SamplePackage@46befbc1
START.HMS=122646
START.MS=1396628806364
START.YMD=20140404
TESTSTART.MS=1396631743509
sunrise=2014-04-04T05:27:38
sunrise_1=2014-04-04T05:27:38
sunrise_matchNr=1
sunset=2014-04-04T18:39:07
sunset_1=2014-04-04T18:39:07
sunset_matchNr=1
wind_dir=West-southwest
wind_dir_1=West-southwest
wind_dir_matchNr=1
```

How it works...

We created a script that made a request to consume a weather API that in turn returned results matching our query in XML format. The details returned included things such as the coordinates of the city, what country the city is in, the temperature, humidity, wind speed, and so on. In our case, the data of concern to us was what direction the wind was blowing at the time we made the request and also what the sunrise and sunset times were for the city. Armed with that information, we constructed and added three XPath Extractors to our test plan, one for each piece of information we needed to extract from the response. We then added a **View Results Tree** listener and **Debug Sampler** to our test plan to ensure we are extracting the intended targets.

 Regular expressions are lower in terms of memory consumption than XPath queries as they don't have to work the DOM the same way the latter has to. Always prefer regular expressions over XPath queries if you have to decide between the two.

There's more...

We have used XPath Extractor in our case, but the same information could be extracted using Regular Expression Extractor. Depending on your needs, you might want to write regular expressions if it suits your needs more. Fortunately, JMeter also comes bundled with an equivalent tester for XPath queries like it does for regular expressions. It is one of the options to select from in the **View Results Tree** listener. Additionally, most major browsers also have plugins that test XPath queries.

Good plugins for Google Chrome and Firefox are listed as follows:

- ▶ **Chrome**: XPath Helper
- ▶ **Firefox**: Firepath Plugin

Both can be installed by searching the respective web stores of the browsers.

With these plugins, you are able to test your XPath queries to see whether they match before transferring them to JMeter.

The XPath syntax is discussed in more detail on http://www.w3schools.com/XPath/xpath_syntax.asp.

Handling JSON responses

When testing most of today's modern web applications, an often-encountered response from the server is a JSON payload. **JSON (JavaScript Object Notation)** is a lightweight data-interchange format that is easy for humans to read/write, and also easy for machines to generate and parse. Due to this ease and its language neutrality, a lot of interchange with servers and services is carried out in this format.

How to do it...

In this recipe, we will cover how to use JMeter to extract information from JSON responses while consuming a freely available weather service. Perform the following steps:

1. Launch JMeter.

2. Add **Thread Group** to the new test plan by navigating to **Test Plan | Add | Threads (Users) | Thread Group**.

3. Add the **HTTP Request** sampler by navigating to **Thread Group | Add | Sampler | HTTP Request**.

4. Fill in its attributes in the following way:

   - **Server Name or IP**: api.openweathermap.org

   - **Method**: GET

   - **Path**: /data/2.5/weather

5. Add the following request parameters to the request by clicking on the **Add** button:

Name	Value
q	London,uk
mode	Json

6. Add three **Regular Expression Extractors** to the **HTTP Request** by navigating to **HTTP Request | Add | Post Processors | Regular Expression Extractor**.

7. Fill in the following details for the three **Regular Expression Extractors** respectively:

Reference name	XPath query	Math no.	Template	Default value
sunrise	"sunrise":(\d+)	0	1	NOT_FOUND
sunset	"sunset":(\d+)	0	1	NOT_FOUND
speed	"speed":([\d.]+)	0	1	NOT_FOUND

8. Add the **View Results Tree** listener to the test plan by navigating to **Test Plan | Add | Listener | View Results Tree**.

9. Add **Debug Sampler** to the test plan by navigating to **Thread Group | Add | Sampler | Debug Sampler**.

10. Save and run the test plan.

11. Observe the results in the **View Results Tree** listener. You should have an output similar to this:

```
{
    "coord":{
        "lon":-76.73,
        "lat":38.94
    },
    "sys":{
        "message":0.0533,
        "country":"US",
        "sunrise":1396694648,
        "sunset":1396740883
    },
    "weather":[
        {
            "id":501,
            "main":"Rain",
            "description":"moderate rain",
            "icon":"10d"
        }
    ],
    "base":"cmc stations",
    "main":{
        "temp":282.25,
        "pressure":1014,
        "humidity":53,
        "temp_min":279.82,
        "temp_max":284.15
    },
    "wind":{
        "speed":7.7,
        "deg":290,
        "gust":13.4
    },
    "rain":{
        "1h":2.29
    },
    "clouds":{
```

```
    "all":1
  },
  "dt":1396702471,
  "id":4349159,
  "name":"Bowie",
  "cod":200
}
```

12. Navigate to **Debug Sampler** and observe our XPath queries matched as expected. Refer to the following code snippet:

```
JMeterVariables:
JMeterThread.last_sample_ok=true
JMeterThread.pack=org.apache.jmeter.threads.
SamplePackage@2ae97e14
START.HMS=053854
START.MS=1396517934834
START.YMD=20140403
TESTSTART.MS=1396702498383
speed=7.7
speed_g=1
speed_g0="speed":7.7
speed_g1=7.7
sunrise=1396694648
sunrise_g=1
sunrise_g0="sunrise":1396694648
sunrise_g1=1396694648
sunset=1396740883
sunset_g=1
sunset_g0="sunset":1396740883
sunset_g1=1396740883
```

How it works...

We created a script that made a request to consume a weather API that in turn returned results matching our query in JSON format. The details returned included things such as the coordinates of the city, what country the city is in, the temperature, humidity, wind speed, and so on. In our case, the data of concern to us was the wind speed at the time we made the request and also what the sunrise and sunset times were for the city. Armed with that information, we constructed and added three Regular Expression Extractors to our test plan, one for each piece of information we needed to extract from the response. We then added a View Results Tree listener and Debug Sampler to our test plan to ensure we are extracting the intended targets.

There's more...

We have used Regular Expression Extractor in our case, but this is by no means the only way you can extract information from a JSON response. As you will see in later recipes, you can extend JMeter with plugins that will provide additional components that ease dealing with more complex JSON structures, for example, the `JSONPathExtractor` plugin on `http://jmeter-plugins.org/wiki/JSONPathExtractor/`.

Some good resources for learning more about JSON are:

- `http://www.json.org/`
- `http://en.wikipedia.org/wiki/JSON`
- `http://www.w3schools.com/json/`

Also, when scripting against web applications that make AJAX calls, the responses from the server are normally in JSON format. One way to monitor traffic and examine the responses of such calls is through the **Network** tab of your browser. This gives you an idea of what the server is returning for each AJAX request and helps prepare the right query or expression to extract the needed information in your script.

The following is a screenshot of what the **Network** tab in the Google Chrome browser looks like when interacting with such an application:

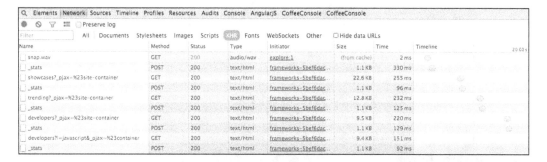

Handling HTML responses

HTML responses are by far the most common responses you will get when scripting against web applications in general. That should come as no surprise since the language of the Web is HTML. HTML DOM elements are used to render all the presentation layer of a website. Since most HTML elements have a beginning and closing tag, for example, `<html></html>`, `<head></head>`, and so on, their structure closely resembles that of XML documents, which we covered in the *Handling XML responses* recipe, and hence they are sometimes referred to as (X)HTML documents. They aren't exactly the same, but it suffices to know they are similar. That said, testing them is very similar to testing XML responses.

How to do it...

In this recipe, we will cover how to use JMeter to extract information from HTML responses. Perform the following steps:

1. Launch JMeter.

2. Add **Thread Group** to the new test plan by navigating to **Test Plan | Add | Threads (Users) | Thread Group**.

3. Add the **HTTP Request** sampler by navigating to **Thread Group | Add | Sampler | HTTP Request**.

4. Fill in its attributes in the following way:

   ❑ **Server Name or IP**: evening-citadel-2263.herokuapp.com

   ❑ **Method**: GET

   ❑ **Path**: N/A

5. Add **CSS/jQuery Extractor** to the **HTTP Request** sampler by navigating to **HTTP Request | Add | Post Processors | CSS/JQuery Extractor**.

6. Fill in the following details for CSS/jQuery Extractor:

   ❑ **Reference Name**: post

   ❑ **CSS/JQuery expression**: div.entry p:matches(\w+)

   ❑ **Attribute**: N/A

   ❑ **Match No**: 0

   ❑ **Default Value**: NOT_FOUND

7. Add **XPath Extractor** to the **HTTP Request** sampler by navigating to **HTTP Request | Add | Post Processors | XPath Extractor**.

8. Fill in the following details for XPath Extractor:

   ❑ **Reference Name**: post_x

   ❑ **XPath query**: /html/body/div/p

   ❑ **Default Value**: NOT_FOUND

9. Add the **View Results Tree** listener to the test plan by navigating to **Test Plan | Add | Listener | View Results Tree**.

10. Add **Debug Sampler** to the test plan by navigating to **Thread Group | Add | Sampler | Debug Sampler**.

11. Save and run the test plan.

12. Observe the results in the **View Results Tree** listener. You should have an output similar to this:

```
<!DOCTYPE html>
<html>
  <body>
    ...
    <div class='entry'>
      <h3>Historic</h3>
      <p>A historic day for @newrelic as we launch Insights
and create a new category: Software Analytics</p>
      <p>Posted by joel</p>
    </div>

    <div class='entry'>
      <h3>Trains</h3>
      <p>WAT? A blog post from @mreinhold that doesn&#39;t
mention trains in the title or atom feed? </p>
      <p>Posted by sam</p>
    </div>

    <div class='entry'>
      <h3>consequat. Duisauteirure dolor in reprehenderit in
voluptatevelitesse</h3>
      <p>I just backed MicroView: Chip-sized Arduino with
built-in OLED Display!</p>
      <p>Posted by hari</p>
    </div>

    <div class='entry'>
      <h3>Thoughts on Scala</h3>
      <p>Must be heavy baby. This and that...</p>
      <p>Posted by bayo</p>
    </div>

    <div class='entry'>
      <h3>Trains</h3>
      <p>WAT? A blog post from @mreinhold that doesn&#39;t
mention trains in the title or atom feed? </p>
      <p>Posted by sam</p>
    </div>
    ...

  </body>
</html>
```

13. Navigate to **Debug Sampler** and observe that our XPath query and CSS/jQuery expression matched as expected. This is shown in the following code:

```
JMeterVariables:
JMeterThread.last_sample_ok=true
JMeterThread.pack=org.apache.jmeter.threads.
SamplePackage@22c81e1d
START.HMS=202355
START.MS=1396743835431
START.YMD=20140405
TESTSTART.MS=1396745910042
post=Must be heavy baby. This and that...
post_x=A historic day for @newrelic as we launch Insights and
create a new category: Software Analytics
post_x_1=A historic day for @newrelic as we launch Insights
and create a new category: Software Analytics
post_x_10=Posted by sam
post_x_2=Posted by joel
post_x_3=WAT? A blog post from @mreinhold that doesn't mention
trains in the title or atom feed?
post_x_4=Posted by sam
post_x_5=I just backed MicroView: Chip-sized Arduino with
built-in OLED Display!
post_x_6=Posted by hari
post_x_7=Must be heavy baby. This and that...
post_x_8=Posted by bayo
post_x_9=WAT? A blog post from @mreinhold that doesn't mention
trains in the title or atom feed?
post_x_matchNr=10
```

How it works...

We created a script that made a request to our test application. The server responded with an HTML document. We then observed the HTML response in the **Elements** tab of our browser to get to grips with its structure (the same can be observed through the **View Results Tree** listener). In our case, we were interested in extracting all the posts made by users from the resulting response. To achieve this, we added an XPath Extractor postprocessor and configured it with a `/html/body/div/p` query, since the observed posts in this particular application are embedded in the HTML paragraph elements. For illustrative purposes, we also added a CSS/jQuery Extractor postprocessor to show how you could get to the same information using that component. However, with CSS/jQuery Extractor, only one random post (since our **Match No** is set to 0) is returned on every invocation.

Finally, we are able to verify our components. We make sure they extract the right things by adding **Debug Sampler** to our test plan and view the results upon executing the test.

There's more...

Though we have used both XPath and CSS/jQuery Extractors in this sample, Regular Expression Extractor could also have been used. Do not feel constrained; employ the right component to get the job done depending on your needs.

See also

- ▸ *The Using Regular Expression Extractor recipe*
- ▸ *The Using Regular Expression Tester recipe*
- ▸ *The Using CSS/jQuery Extractor recipe*
- ▸ *The Using XPath Extractor recipe*
- ▸ *The Handling XML responses recipe*

Using Response Assertion

JMeter comes bundled with assertion components. Assertions are used to perform additional checks on samplers and are processed by default after every sampler in the same scope, except for in cases where they have been added as a direct child of a sampler. You can think of these as mini unit tests within your test plans that ensure the responses from the server actually work fine. For example, when you make HTTP requests in a web application, the server responses may respond with different HTTP header status codes, denoting the success or failure of your request. A status code of 200, for example, means the request succeeded, 401 means access was denied to the requested resource, 500 means an internal server error occurred while attempting to fulfill your request, and so on.

How to do it...

In this recipe, we will cover how to use JMeter's Response Assertion to provide our test scripts with additional checks, thus making them more robust. Perform the following steps:

1. Launch JMeter.
2. Add **Thread Group** to the new test plan by navigating to **Test Plan | Add | Threads (Users) | Thread Group**.
3. Add the **HTTP Request** sampler by navigating to **Thread Group | Add | Sampler | HTTP Request**.

4. Fill in its attributes in the following way:

   ❑ **Server Name or IP**: `evening-citadel-2263.herokuapp.com`

   ❑ **Method**: `GET`

   ❑ **Path**: N/A

5. Add the **Response Assertion** component to the **HTTP Request** sampler by navigating to **HTTP Request | Add | Assertions | Response Assertion**.

6. Add the following pattern to match the output:

   ```
   <a href='/logout'>logout</a>
   ```

7. Add the **View Results Tree** listener by navigating to **Test Plan | Add | Listener | View Results Tree**.

8. Save and run the test.

9. Observe that the assertion fails.

10. Add the following four patterns separately by clicking on the **Add** button four times:

    ```
    <body>
    Posted by
    <a href='/login'>login</a>
    <a href='/register'>register</a>
    ```

11. Save and re-run the test.

12. Notice that the request succeeds including the assertion checks, as shown in the following screenshot:

How it works...

We constructed a simple test plan that made a single request to a web application returning its home page. We then added a Response Assertion component to the HTTP request to run additional checks on the server response. In our first trial, we purposely ran a check that was bound to fail (looking for a logout link when the user had not logged in) to verify the assertion was actually doing its job. Once that was confirmed, we deleted the failed check and added four additional pattern checks to assert. This included checking there is at least one post on the site, whether registered links are present if the user is not logged in, and so on. We then re-ran our test and observed a successful run.

 Assertions have a performance impact on test execution, so try to avoid using too many (more than a couple) within your test plans.

There's more...

In our case, we are asserting the text response from the server. Response Assertion can be used to assert URLs, response code, response messages, and response headers. In addition, it can be configured to do contains, matches, equals, or substring searches. This can be very helpful depending on your use case and how you intend to assert.

Using Duration Assertion

Another useful assertion component that comes bundled with JMeter is the Duration Assertion component. Like its name implies, this component is used to test that each response returns within a given time specified by the user. Any response that doesn't return within the specified time is marked as a failed response. For example, this can be particularly useful when testing API calls for application services, or ensuring the accumulative service calls to render a page are all performing efficiently.

How to do it...

In this recipe, we will cover how to use the Duration Assertion component. Perform the following steps:

1. Launch JMeter.
2. Add **Thread Group** to the new test plan by navigating to **Test Plan | Add | Threads (Users) | Thread Group**.
3. Add the **HTTP Request** sampler by navigating to **Thread Group | Add | Sampler | HTTP Request**.

4. Fill in its attributes in the following way:

   ❑ **Server Name or IP**: `evening-citadel-2263.herokuapp.com`

   ❑ **Method**: `GET`

   ❑ **Path**: N/A

5. Add the **Duration Assertion** component to the **HTTP Request** sampler by navigating to **HTTP Request | Add | Assertions | Duration Assertion**.

6. In the **Duration in milliseconds** box, enter `50`.

7. Add the **View Results Tree** listener by navigating to **Test Plan | Add | Listener | View Results Tree**.

8. Save and run the test.

9. Observe that the assertion fails. You should see a failure similar to the one shown in **View Results Tree**, as follows:

   ```
   Assertion error: false
   Assertion failure: true
   Assertion failure message: The operation lasted too long: It took
   5,756 milliseconds, but should not have lasted longer than 50
   milliseconds.
   ```

10. Increase **Duration in milliseconds** (in step 6) to `5000`.

11. Save and re-run the test.

12. Observe that the assertion now succeeds.

How it works...

Once added to a request, the Duration Assertion component verifies that the response to which it is applied comes back in the time specified by the user. Responses that come back within the time specified are considered successful while those that lapse are failed.

There's more...

This can be used in conjunction with other assertion components, for example, the Response Assertion component we covered in the previous recipe (*Using Duration Assertion*). We encourage you to look at `http://jmeter.apache.org/usermanual/component_reference.html#assertions` for a complete list of assertion components bundled with JMeter.

Uploading files with your scripts

Uploading files is a common functionality in web applications. Social networks, for example, encourage you to upload a profile picture when registering for an account. Attaching files to e-mails is also a fairly common routine task. Services such as Dropbox allow you to upload multiple files through their web and platform-native applications. JMeter allows you to test such applications by providing a mechanism to upload files as part of your test plan. In this recipe, we will cover how to upload files with JMeter.

How to do it...

Perform the following steps to upload files with your scripts:

1. Launch JMeter.
2. Add **HTTP(S) Test Script Recorder** by navigating to **WorkBench | Add | Non-Test Elements | HTTP Mirror Server** and configure it appropriately.
3. Start the HTTP(S) Test Script Recorder.
4. Point your browser to `http://angular-file-upload.appspot.com/`.
5. Click on the **Choose File** button to choose a single text file.
6. Choose a file to upload.
7. Stop the script recorder.
8. Add the **View Results Tree** listener to the test plan by navigating to **Test Plan | Add | Listener | View Results Tree**.
9. Save and run the test plan.
10. Observe the results.

How it works...

To upload files, HTML form elements require a post action with multipart / form-data content or a MIME type (content-type). JMeter comes bundled with a built-in multipart / form-data option for post requests, enabling it to correctly process file uploads. We leveraged this option in step 6 when we uploaded a file through the web application.

JMeter assumes the file we are uploading resides in the `bin` directory or paths relative to the `bin` directory. You either need to specify the absolute path of the file in your script or put it in the expected directory. Failure to do this will lead to errors (for example, `java.io.FileNotFoundException: bg.jpg` (no such file or directory)) when re-executing the script after recording it.

There's more...

If you observe the recorded request for the actual file upload, you will notice all it is doing is marking a post to use multipart / form-data and then specifying the file path of the file, parameter name, and MIME type. The MIME type allows the appropriate type to be set for different file types, for example, PDF, image, text, doc, and so on. For example, we could go further and use this in conjunction with the concepts we covered in the *Dealing with file downloads* recipe and test an end-to-end file transfer from one application to another.

3
Building Robust Test Plans with Controllers

In this chapter, we will cover the following recipes:

- ▶ Using Transaction Controller in test plans
- ▶ Using Loop Controller in test plans
- ▶ Leveraging ForEach Controller in test plans
- ▶ Using Interleave and Random Controllers in test plans
- ▶ Using Runtime Controller in test plans

Introduction

Whether you are recording scripts or manually writing them, you will need to make use of controllers to aid the logic within your test plan. Logic controllers help determine the order in which samplers are processed in your test plans. Controllers are direct child elements of a Thread Group and contain one or more samplers. There are various controllers ranging from logic (random, if, switch, and so on) to looping (while, ForEach, loop, and so on), and recording controllers. At the time of writing this, JMeter comes bundled with 16 different controllers; more controllers can be provided by extending JMeter with plugins.

In this chapter, we will detail how to use five of the most frequently encountered controllers in the test plans. Due to page constraints, we are unable to cover all controllers. For a full list of bundled controllers including those not covered in this chapter's recipes, visit `http://jmeter.apache.org/usermanual/component_reference.html#logic_controllers`.

Using Transaction Controller in test plans

In general, you can think of controllers as container elements that group or hold numerous samplers. Transaction controllers are a specialized form of controllers that generate an additional sample that measures the overall time taken to perform its nested samplers. For instance, in most typical web applications, it takes a number of requests to provide all the data needed for a page to render correctly. This could involve several AJAX calls to the backend server or external web services. For such circumstances, you might be interested in how long it takes for the combined set of requests to execute, and not just for individual ones.

How to do it...

In this recipe, we will cover how to use Transaction Controllers to measure the combined time taken for a series of requests that satisfy the operation. Perform the following steps:

1. Launch JMeter.

2. Click on the **Templates...** button (right next to the **New** button) on the toolbar.

3. Select **Recording** from the **Select Template** drop-down and click on the **Create** button.

4. Under **WorkBench**, click on the **HTTP(S) Test Script Recorder** and do the following:

    ❏ **Port**: 7070 (or your desired proxy port)

    ❏ **URL Patterns to Exclude**: .*\.(bmp|css|js|gif|ico|jpe?g|png|swf|woff).*

> Refer to the *Recording a script via HTTP(S) Test Script Recorder* recipe in *Chapter 1, JMeter Fundamentals,* for details on how this is done.

5. Click on the **Start** button and accept the CA certification to begin the script recorder.

6. Open your browser and configure it to use the recorder you set up in step 4.

> Refer to the *Recording a script via HTTP(S) Test Script Recorder* recipe in *Chapter 1, JMeter Fundamentals,* for details on how this is done.

7. Point your browser to `http://www.huffingtonpost.com` (or any website of your choice).

8. Browse around the website a little.

9. Stop the script recorder.

10. Observe the recorded test plan.

11. Add **Aggregate Report** listener to the test plan by navigating to **Test Plan | Add | Listener | Aggregate Report**.

12. Save and run the test plan. Notice that the individual request times are reported individually.

13. For each Transaction Controller, check the **Generate parent sample** checkbox.

14. Save and run the test plan and notice that the parent sampler is now recorded (not the individual ones). This is shown in the following screenshot:

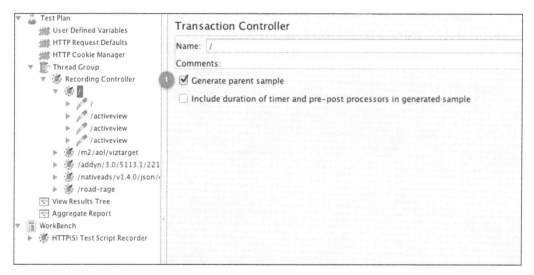

Generating parent sampler times with Transaction Controller

The recorded test plan for this recipe is bundled with the book under the name `ch3_tx_ctrl.jmx`. Alternatively, you can download or clone the test plan from the `Git` repository for the book at `https://github.com/jmeter-cookbook/bundled-code`.

How it works...

To serve up a page in most web applications, a number of calls to services might be needed to gather all the information needed by the page. This is normally accomplished through asynchronous requests to those services via **AJAX (Asynchronous JavaScript and XML)** calls. It is the duty of Transaction Controller to bundle all such related calls into a single transaction, so that the total time taken to satisfy all such calls can be measured cumulatively.

In our use case, in step 4, we instructed the script recorder to group all related calls into new transactions. With the browser configured to use the proxy in step 6, we then proceeded to our web application in step 7. As we navigated through various pages within the application, all the requests needed to satisfy each page are grouped into separate Transaction Controllers. Once we had our various transaction groups, we were then about to measure the individual execution times for each sampler in step 14. However, since we were interested in how long it took to execute all requests within a page, we checked the **Generate parent sample** checkbox in each Transaction Controller and re-ran the test script. This gave us the summarized view of how long it took for each page to load. This is demonstrated in the following screenshot:

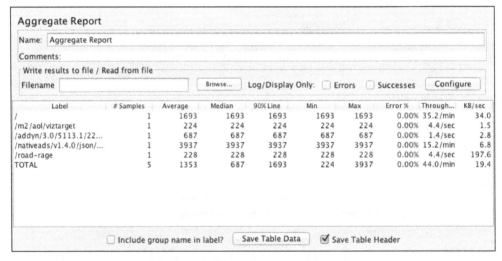

Using Aggregate Report to view summary results

There's more...

It is important to note that the Transaction Controller records all time spent by nested samplers excluding any timers included as part of the thread group or controller. So for instance, if we had a constant timer that paused for say half a second (500 milliseconds), then that time is not included as part of the total execution time of the Transaction Controller. If you would like to take those into account, check the **Include duration of timer** and pre-post processors in **Generated parent sample** checkbox for each Transaction Controller in your test plan.

Using Loop Controller in test plans

Sometimes when testing applications, you might need to repeatedly execute a particular request or group of requests for a certain number of times over a given period. For example, simulating a user paging through the various posts for a blog, going through their monthly transaction activities on a financial website, or paging through the search results of matching products on an e-commerce website, and so on. For all these cases, Loop Controllers come to the rescue.

Loop Controllers are controllers that specialize in executing all their contained child samplers repeatedly for a given number of times. They are a perfect fit for the paging scenarios described previously.

How to do it...

In this recipe, we will cover how to use Loop Controllers to perform repeated tasks within a test plan. Perform the following steps:

1. Launch JMeter.
2. Click on the **Templates...** button (right next to the **New** button) on the toolbar.
3. Select **Recording** from the **Select Template** drop-down and click on the **Create** button.
4. Under **WorkBench**, click on the **HTTP(S) Test Script Recorder** and do the following:
    - **Port**: 7070 (or your desired proxy port)
    - **URL Patterns to Exclude**: .*\.(bmp|css|js|gif|ico|jpe?g|png|swf|woff).*

> Refer to the *Recording a script via HTTP(S) Test Script Recorder* recipe in *Chapter 1, JMeter Fundamentals*, for details on how this is done.

5. Click on the **Start** button and accept the CA certification to begin the script recorder.

6. Open your browser and configure it to use the recorder you set up in step 4.

> Refer to the *Recording a script via HTTP(S) Test Script Recorder* recipe in *Chapter 1, JMeter Fundamentals*, for details on how this is done.

7. Point your browser to http://evening-citadel-2263.herokuapp.com.
8. Click on the **Next** link three times.
9. Click on the **Previous** link three times.
10. Stop the script recorder.
11. Observe the recorded test plan.
12. Save and run the test plan. Observe the results of the execution.
13. Add **Loop Controller** to the **Sampler** produced in step 8 by navigating to **Sampler | Insert Parent | Logic Controller | Loop Controller**.

> In this step, you are grouping three samplers under a Loop Controller. See the following screenshot for what the final output should look like.

14. Add a Loop Controller to the sample produced in step 9 by navigating to **Sampler | Insert Parent | Logic Controller | Loop Controller**.
15. For both Loop Controllers added, specify a loop count of 2.
16. Save and run the test plan. Observe the results of the execution. This is shown in the following screenshot:

> The recorded test plan for this recipe is bundled with the book under the name ch3_loop_ctrl.jmx. Alternatively, you can download or clone them from the Git repository for the book at https://github.com/jmeter-cookbook/bundled-code.

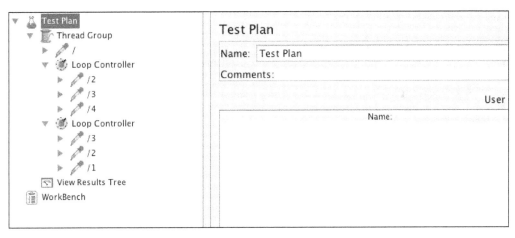

Using Loop Controllers

The following screenshot shows how to specify the number of loops in the Loop Controller component:

Loop Controller

Name: Loop Controller

Comments:

Loop Count: ☐ Forever 2 ⬅

Specifying the loop count for a Loop Controller

How it works...

What we intended to achieve on the outset of this recipe was to use JMeter to simulate a user browsing a sample blog post site page by page. Instead of recording each pagination link click, for example, viewing the next three pages by clicking next link three times, we just clicked on the next link only once in step 8. We also recorded a previous link by clicking the same way. We then added two Loop Controllers to our test plan; one as the parent component of the next samplers and the other that of the previous samplers. This gives us the flexibility to control the number of times we execute each sampler individually. With that, we are now able to fully simulate the scenario we set out to emulate; a user paging through posts on a website.

This is shown in the following screenshot:

Since embedded components, samplers, timers, functions, and so on are executed repeatedly for as many times as defined in the Loop Controller, you should be mindful of their side effects. For example, functions such as `random` will get a new value upon each loop execution.

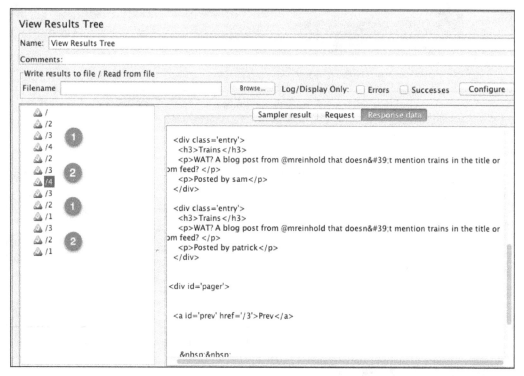

Results denoting that four iterations were run

There's more...

Loop Controller components have a checkbox named **Forever**. Like its name implies, this property when checked puts the controller into an infinite loop. Child components of the Loop Controller are executed continuously until the test plan is forcefully stopped. This can be helpful when running stress testing on a system or application.

Loop Controllers can also be combined with other forms of controllers in the same test plan to give the desired simulated scenarios.

▶ **While Controller**: https://jmeter.apache.org/usermanual/component_ reference.html#While_Controller

▶ **ForEach Controller**: https://jmeter.apache.org/usermanual/component_ reference.html#ForEach_Controller

Leveraging ForEach Controller in test plans

Another variation of Loop Controllers you might sometimes encounter is the ForEach controller. These are a specialized form of controllers that loop through the values of a set of related values. The number of iteration execution is dynamically defined by the resolution of the related variables as opposed to a fixed number specified in loop controllers. This makes ForEach Controllers a good fit for use cases where you need to perform repetitive executions of samplers based on some information from the target application.

How to do it...

In this recipe, we will cover how to use ForEach controllers paginating through the posts of our sample application. This is going to be very similar to what was covered in the *Using Loop Controller in test plans* recipe, only this time, we will use the ForEach Controller to give you an idea of how it can be used to achieve a similar result. Perform the following steps:

1. Launch JMeter.
2. Click on the **Templates...** button (right next to the **New** button) on the toolbar.
3. Select **Recording** from the **Select Template** drop-down and click on the **Create** button.
4. Under **WorkBench**, click on **HTTP(S) Test Script Recorder** and update the following parameters:

    ❑ **Port**: 7070 (or your desired proxy port)

    ❑ **URL Patterns to Exclude**: .*\.(bmp|css|js|gif|ico|jpe?g|png|swf |woff).*

 Refer to the *Recording a script via HTTP(S) Test Script Recorder* recipe in *Chapter 1, JMeter Fundamentals*, for details on how this is done.

5. Click on the **Start** button and accept the CA certification to begin the script recorder.
6. Open your browser and configure it to use the recorder you set up in step 4.

7. Point your browser to `http://evening-citadel-2263.herokuapp.com`.

8. Click on the **Next** link.

9. Click on the **Previous** link.

10. Stop the script recorder.

11. Add **ForEach Controller** as the parent of the sampler produced in step 8 by navigating to **Transaction Controller | Change Controller | Logic Controller | ForEach Controller**.

12. Add **ForEach Controller** as the parent of the samplers produced in step 9 by navigating to **Transaction Controller | Change Controller | Logic Controller | ForEach Controller**.

13. Update the first ForEach Controller with the following details:
    - **Input variable prefix**: `page`
    - **Output variable name**: `returnPage`

14. Update the second ForEach Controller with the following details:
    - **Input variable prefix**: `prev`
    - **Output variable name**: `returnPage`

15. Update the name and path of the child samplers (HTTP Request) of the ForEach controllers to the following:
    - **Name**: `/${returnPage}`
    - **Path**: `/${returnPage}`

16. Add two **User Defined Variables** components to the thread group by navigating to **Thread Group | Config Element | User Defined Variables**.

17. Add the following entries to the first **User Defined Variables** component:

Name	Value	Description
`page_1`	1	N/A
`page_2`	2	N/A
`page_3`	3	N/A
`page_4`	4	N/A

18. Add the following entries to the second **User Defined Variables** component:

Name	Value	Description
`prev_1`	4	N/A
`prev_2`	3	N/A
`prev_3`	2	N/A
`prev_4`	1	N/A

19. Add a **View Results Tree** listener to your test plan by navigating to **Test Plan | Add | Listener | View Results Tree**.

20. Save and run the test plan. Observe the results of the execution.

> The recorded test plan for this recipe is bundled with the book under the name `ch3_foreach_ctrl.jmx`. Alternatively, you can download or clone the test plan from the `Git` repository for the book at `https://github.com/jmeter-cookbook/bundled-code`.

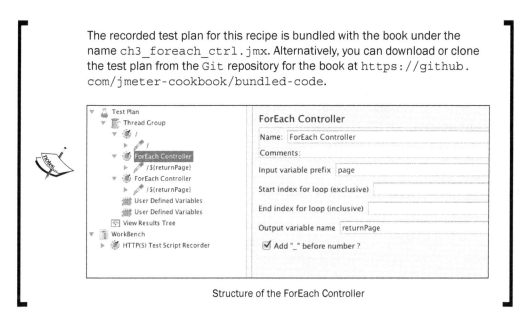

Structure of the ForEach Controller

The following screenshot shows how to specify variables in the **User Defined Variables** component:

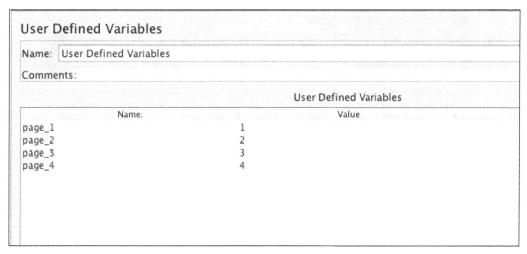

User defined variables

How it works...

First, we recorded our sample scenario of a user browsing our sample application. Once recorded, we put each of the pagination links within a ForEach Controller. We then added a **User Defined Variables** component to our test plan defining the variables page_1 to page_4 with input values for our ForEach Controller component to consume. Since we defined our input variable prefix as Page and output variable as returnPage in the ForEach controller, on each iteration, the controller reads a page_x or prev_x (where x is the iteration count) value and produces a different value in the returnPage. In the embedded child HTTP Samplers, we then use the value contained in the returnPage variable to dynamically feed data into the sampler.

There's more...

In addition to using **User Defined Variables** with the ForEach controller, postprocessors such as Regular Expression Extractor, CSS/jQuery Extractor, XPath Extractor, and so on can be used to process the preceding HTTP Samplers, and used to define values to feed into the ForEach component. If possible, this is actually a better alternative to using **User Defined Variables** as they make feed values completely dynamic based on the application.

See also

▸ http://jmeter.apache.org/demos/ForEachTest2.jmx
▸ http://jmeter.apache.org/demos/forEachTestPlan.jmx

Using Interleave and Random Controller in test plans

When designing test plans, sometimes it is useful to simulate the random behavior of users. That is, not have all users in your test plan execute the same flow of events in the same manner. For example, in a typical e-commerce website selling products, it is not unusual to have potential consumers come and shop for different products. Some visit the site with the intention of buying, while some might have just visited the site to compare prices with a competing vendor. So, you could have Consumer A visit the site, browse around, put a few items in their cart, and then check out. Consumer B visits the site, just browses, not adding anything to their cart. As such, for this described scenario, we have two scenarios that we could interleave or randomly pick between.

JMeter provides two built-in controllers that allow us to do just that. These are Interleave and Random Controllers. These two controllers closely resemble each other in functionality. Interleave Controllers allow JMeter to alternate between child components on each iteration pass. Random Controllers, on the other hand, allow JMeter to randomly pick the child component to execute on each iteration pass. As such, the processing order of an Interleave Controller is predetermined based on the number of iterations specified, while that of a random controller is not. So for example, for a Random Controller contained in a thread group with one thread and six loops with say six child samplers, it is possible that only three or four of the samplers are executed during a single execution run, while the others are not because they were not randomly picked. However, for an Interleave Controller, under the same defined conditions, all child elements are guaranteed to be executed.

In this recipe, we will cover how to use controllers in a test plan.

How to do it...

In this recipe, we will cover how to use both Interleave and Random Controllers in a test plan. Perform the following steps:

1. Launch JMeter.
2. Click on the **Templates...** button (right next to the **New** button) on the toolbar.
3. Select **Recording** from the **Select Template** dropdown and click on the **Create** button.
4. Under **WorkBench**, click on the **HTTP(S) Test Script Recorder** and do the following:
   - **Port**: 7070 (or your desired proxy port)
   - **URL Patterns to Exclude**: .*\.(bmp|css|js|gif|ico|jpe?g|png|swf|woff).*

 Refer to the *Recording a script via HTTP(S) Test Script Recorder* recipe in *Chapter 1, JMeter Fundamentals*, for details on how this is done.

5. Click on the **Start** button and accept the CA certification to begin the script recorder.
6. Open your browser and configure it to use the recorder you set up in step 4.
7. Point your browser to http://evening-citadel-2263.herokuapp.com.
8. Click on the **Next** link once.
9. Click on the **Previous** link once.
10. Click on the **Login** link in the top right corner.
11. Log in to the application with valid credentials (**Username**: bayo and **Password**: express).
12. Click on the **Post** link.

13. Fill in the details of the post and submit.

14. Click the **Logout** link to log out of the application.

15. Stop the script recorder.

16. Observe the recorded test plan.

17. Save and run the test plan. Observe the results of the execution.

18. Add **Interleave Controller** to the sample produced in steps 8 and 9 by navigating to **Sampler | Add | Insert Parent | Logic Controller | Interleave Controller**.

19. Add **Interleave Controller** as the parent of the samplers produced from steps 10 to 13 by navigating to **Sampler | Add | Insert Parent | Logic Controller | Interleave Controller**.

20. Save and run the test plan. Observe the results of the execution.

21. Replace the Interleave Controller with a Random Controller by navigating to **Sampler | Add | Insert Parent | Logic Controller | Random Controller**.

22. Save and run the test plan. Observe the results of the execution.

The recorded test plans for this recipe are bundled with the book under the names `ch3_interleave_ctrl.jmx` and `ch3_random_ctrl.jmx` respectively. Alternatively, you can download or clone them from the `Git` repository for the book at `https://github.com/jmeter-cookbook/bundled-code`.

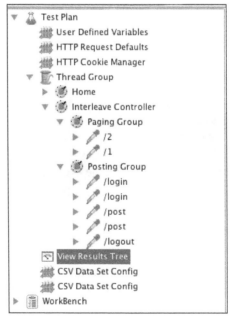

Using the Interleave Controller

The following screenshot shows how your test plan should be laid out when using a Random Controller for our previous example:

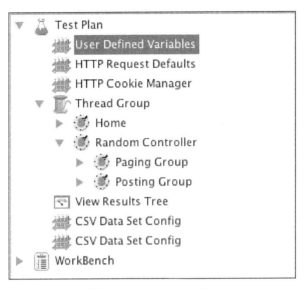

Using the Random Controller

How it works...

We recorded two scenarios in our test plan: a user browsing posts in our sample application and one that posted a message. We then post both these samplers under an Interleave Controller. Once the Interleave Controller was added, we saved and executed the test plan. What we observe is that the browse and post samplers are alternately executed for our specified loop iteration. That is, browse, post, browse, post, and then browse since we only specified five loops in our thread group.

We then swapped the Interleave Controller for a Random Controller, saved, and repeated the test run. This time, we observed that browse and post samplers are executed at random and not interleaved. For our case, we had only the post flow executed for the same specified loop of five iterations.

This is shown in the following screenshot:

Since each embedded component, samplers, timer, functions, and so on are executed repeatedly for as many times as defined in the loop controller, you should be mindful of their side effects. For example, functions such as `random` will get a new value upon each loop execution.

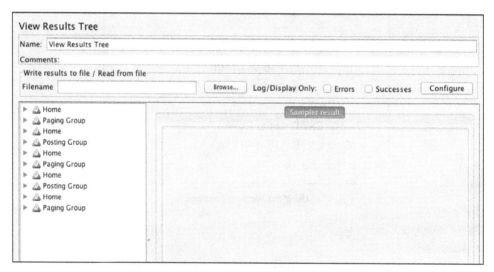

Flow of execution with Interleave Controller

The following screenshot shows the results of executing the test with a Random Controller Component:

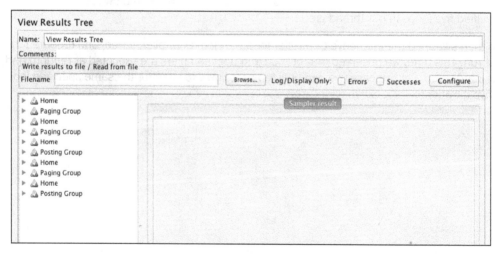

Flow of execution with Random Controller

There's more...

Both Interleave and Random Controller components have a checkbox named **Ignore sub-controller block** which, once checked, allows you to skip execution of all subcomponents embedded within them. This is helpful to quickly ignore a group of samplers and child components. In addition, both these controllers can be used in combination with user controllers in JMeter.

Using Runtime Controller in test plans

When designing test plans, sometimes it is useful to have control over the duration of execution for the various samplers contained within your test plan. It might be helpful to run a particular group of requests longer than others to see what stress the requests put on the system. This is exactly what the Runtime Controller does. It allows us to control how long its child elements are allowed to run for. This can help shape our test plans to mimic the actual behavior of users in our system. For example, on a typical blogging website, there is far more time spent reading the contents of posts by readers than there is putting up new posts. As a result, you may want the reading flow to execute for half an hour, while the posting flow executes for only 5 minutes.

How to do it...

In this recipe, we will cover the usage of a Runtime Controller. Perform the following steps:

1. Launch JMeter.
2. Click on the **Templates...** button (right next to the **New** button) on the toolbar.
3. Select **Recording** from the **Select Template** drop-down and click on the **Create** button.
4. Under **WorkBench**, click on the **HTTP(S) Test Script Recorder** and update the following parameters:

    ❑ **Port**: 7070 (or your desired proxy port)

    ❑ **URL Patterns to Exclude**: .*\.(bmp|css|js|gif|ico|jpe?g|png|swf|woff).*

 Refer to the *Recording a script via HTTP(S) Test Script Recorder* recipe in *Chapter 1, JMeter Fundamentals*, for details on how this is done.

5. Click on the **Start** button and accept the CA certification to begin the script recorder.
6. Open your browser and configure it to use the recorder you set up in step 4.

7. Point your browser to `http://evening-citadel-2263.herokuapp.com`.

8. Click on the **Next** link three times.

9. Click on the **Previous** link three times.

10. Stop the script recorder.

11. Observe the recorded test plan.

12. Save and run the test plan. Observe the results of the execution.

13. Add **Loop Controller** to the sample produced in step 8 by navigating to **HTTP Request | Insert Parent | Logic Controller | Loop Controller**.

14. Add **Loop Controller** to the sample produced in step 9 by navigating to **HTTP Request | Insert Parent | Logic Controller | Loop Controller**.

15. Add **Runtime Controller** as a parent of both samplers produced in step 8 and 9 by navigating to **Loop Controller | Insert Parent | Logic Controller | Runtime Controller**.

16. In the Runtime Controller, specify a time of `60` seconds (that is, `1` minute).

17. Save and run the test plan. Observe the number of times each sampler ran during the specified minute execution. This is shown in the following screenshot:

 The recorded test plans for this recipe are bundled with the book under the name `ch3_runtime_ctrl.jmx`. Alternatively, you can download or clone the test plan from the `Git` repository for the book at `https://github.com/jmeter-cookbook/bundled-code`.

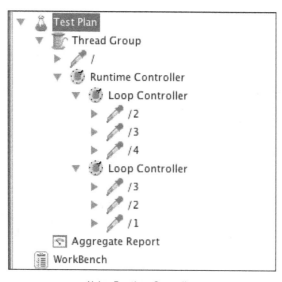

Using Runtime Controller

How it works...

We recorded a scenario of a user simply browsing our sample website. Once done, we put some of the recorded samplers into loops in steps 14 and 15 to simulate the user paging through the listed posts on the website. We then embedded the pagination flows within a Runtime Controller. Having these components under the Runtime Controller allows us to control how long they can run for. In our case, we have chosen to have them run for a minute. Once configured, we saved the test plan and we were able to observe from the result listener that the test execution reflected just that.

There's more...

Runtime Controllers give us a handle on controlling just how long parts of our test plan or entire test plan should run. Their child subcomponents can be any of JMeter's built-in samplers or controllers like we had in our example previously. Also, like with most controllers, it can be used in combination with other components (built-in and extended) to help shape your desired scenarios.

4
Testing Services

In this chapter, we will cover the following topics:

- ▶ Testing REST web services
- ▶ Testing SOAP web services
- ▶ Testing FTP services
- ▶ Testing relational databases
- ▶ Testing NoSQL databases
- ▶ Testing JMS services

Introduction

Services are the heartbeat of any application because of the critical role they play in the entire application. They are also responsible for orchestrating communications between the controllers and lower-level resources such as the database, messaging resources, third-party services, and so on. Furthermore, they often encapsulate the business logic of the application, thereby doing most of the heavy lifting so to speak. As such, it is important to have a means of testing them and knowing whether they pose a bottleneck to the application or not. Testing them could help expose areas that need tuning within the application or infrastructure that could then be communicated to the responsible parties.

Apart from testing services, it is also beneficial to test the underlying resources the application relies on directly. Such resources could be the database, messaging, e-mail, ftp, reporting, and so on.

In this chapter, we will detail how to test two categories of services, REST and SOAP. In later recipes, we cover how to directly test the database, ftp, and messaging resources.

Testing REST web services

Representational State Transfer (**REST**) is an architectural style of designing network applications that relies on a stateless client-server and cacheable communications protocol (HTTP). Compared to alternatives such as **Remote Procedure Calls** (**RPC**), **Simple Object Access Protocol** (**SOAP**), and so on, REST is lightweight, mainly because all communications between the client and server are over HTTP. This makes them easily testable as well.

REST web services adhere to the principles of REST and rely on the following HTTP methods: GET, PUT, POST, and DELETE. GET is used to list or retrieve resource(s), PUT is used to replace or update resource(s), POST is used to create a new resource, and DELETE is used to delete resource(s). Since REST is an architectural style and not a protocol, there is no official standard. The only constraints are to stick to the guidelines laid out by REST.

How to do it...

In this recipe, we will cover how to test REST web services. Perform the following steps:

1. Launch JMeter.

2. Add **Thread Group** by navigating to **Test Plan | Add | Threads(Users) | Thread Group**.

3. Add the **HTTP Request Default** component by navigating to **Thread Group | Add | Config Element | HTTP Request Default**. Update the following details:

    ❑ **Server Name or IP**: api-jcb.herokuapp.com

4. Add the **HTTP Header Manager** component by navigating to **Thread Group | Add | Config Element | HTTP Header Manager**.

5. Click on the **Add** button to add a header attribute. Update the following details:

    ❑ **Name**: Content-Type

    ❑ **Value**: application/json

6. Add **HTTP Request** to **Thread Group** by navigating to **Thread Group | Add | Sampler | HTTP Request**. Update the following details:

    ❑ **Name**: Get All Requests

    ❑ **Path**: /holiday-requests

7. Add another **HTTP Request** to **Thread Group** by navigating to **Thread Group | Add | Sampler | HTTP Request**. Update the following details:

    ❑ **Name**: Create Holiday Request

    ❑ **Path**: /holiday-requests

- **Method**: POST
- **Body Data**: This is given by the following code snippet:

```
{
  "employeeId": 688,
  "employeeName": "Stephen Lee",
  "startDate": "2014-07-01T00:00:00Z",
  "endDate": "2014-07-08T00:00:00Z"
}
```

8. Add **Regular Expression Extractor** to the **Create Holiday Request** HTTP sampler by navigating to **Create Holiday Request | Add | Post Processor | Regular Expression Extractor**.

9. Fill in the details for **Regular Expression Extractor** as follows:

- **Reference Name**: id
- **Regular Expression**: "id":(\d+)
- **Template**: 1
- **Match No.**: 0
- **Default Value**: NOT_FOUND

10. Add another **HTTP Request** to **Thread Group** by navigating to **Thread Group | Add | Sampler | HTTP Request**. Fill in the following details:

- **Name**: Modify Holiday
- **Path**: /holiday-requests
- **Method**: PUT
- **Body Data**: This is given by the following code snippet:

```
{
        "id":${id},
        "employeeId": 688,
        "employeeName": "Stephen Lee",
         "startDate": "2014-08-01T00:00:00Z",
          "endDate": "2014-08-08T00:00:00Z"
}
```

11. Add another **HTTP Request** to **Thread Group** by navigating to **Thread Group | Add | Sampler | HTTP Request**. Fill in the following details:

- **Name**: Delete Holiday
- **Path**: /holiday-requests/${id}
- **Method**: DELETE

12. Add the **View Results Tree** listener to the test plan by navigating to **Test Plan | Add | Listener | View Results Tree**.

13. Save and run the test plan. Observe the results of the execution.

 The recorded test plan for this recipe is bundled with the book under the name `ch4-rest.jmx`. Alternatively, it can be downloaded or cloned from the book's Git repository at `http://github.com/jmeter-cookbook/bundled-code`.

How it works...

As stated earlier, REST services almost always operate over a HTTP protocol. This makes the **HTTP Request** component a viable option to test them. In our scenario, we are testing a Human Resources web service. The Human Resources department of a company, for example, will be the consumer of the service, using it to manage employee vacation requests. Through this service, employees of a company can put in vacation requests (POST). They can update the details of the requests should they later change their mind (PUT). They could altogether cancel the vacation (DELETE). At any given point, we can see a list of all the holiday requests that have been put in or even narrow down on a particular one (GET).

To test all these scenarios, we created a new test plan, added **Thread Group** to it, and added **HTTP Request** as a child component of **Thread Group**. For reuse, we added the **HTTP Request Defaults** and **HTTP Header Manager** components to **Thread Group**. The former allows us to define common elements such as the host server, port, request parameters, and so on. The latter allows us to provide additional arguments or parameters to **HTTP Header**. This is not to be confused with request parameters. In our case, our service retrieves and sends JSON, so we add a single entry, **Content-Type**: `application/json`. The **Content-Type** represents the MIME type of the **HTTP Request** body and is used to denote the content of HTTP POST and PUT requests. With those set, we consume our service to retrieve some resources from a URI. To do this, we configured the path of the **HTTP Request** component we added to `/holiday-requests`. This takes care of getting all vacations requested by employees. If we wanted to narrow this down and get a particular vacation, we could instead have used `/holiday-requests/id`, where `id` is the identifier of the target vacation.

In the same manner, we provided requests to create, update, and delete a resource in steps 7, 10, and 11 respectively. We accomplished this by adding **HTTP Request** samplers to **Thread Group** with the right HTTP methods accordingly. To create a new resource, we used POST and sent the JSON representing the resource we wanted to create with **HTTP Request**. To update a resource, we used PUT and sent the updated resource with the request in JSON format. Finally, to delete the resource, we sent a HTTP request to `/holiday-requests/id` with a DELETE method, where `id` represented the resource to delete.

There's more...

It is not uncommon to encounter REST web services that are securely protected. Attempting to invoke such services without proper credentials will lead to an access denied error. As such, we have to properly send across the credentials with each request we make to such secure services. Often, this can be accomplished by adding **HTTP Header** properties representing validation tokens along with each request. Just like we added a header property to denote we will be receiving and sending JSON messages to our service, we can add additional header properties to represent such tokens. These tokens vary from service to service, so be sure to consult the API vendor for the valid properties to set when testing them. HTTP basic authentication and OAuth are the standard REST security mechanisms and can both be handled through the **HTTP Header** properties.

See also

More information about REST can be found at
`http://en.wikipedia.org/wiki/Representational_state_transfer`.

Testing SOAP web services

SOAP is a protocol specification to exchange information between network systems. Communication and negotiation between systems is done by passing XML message formats over a variety of transport protocols, including HTTP, JMS, Mail, VFS, and so on. Unlike REST, which is an architectural style, SOAP is a protocol, and is thus governed by standards. Due to SOAP's characteristics (extensibility, neutrality, and independence), it is a good candidate for systems integration and interoperability. It provides a mechanism for legacy and modern systems to communicate effectively without needing to be on the same platform or in the same programming language.

JMeter offers two components (SOAP/XML-RPC Request and HTTP Request) that help when testing SOAP web services.

How to do it...

In this recipe, we will see how both SOAP/XML-RPC and HTTP Request can be used to test SOAP web services:

1. Launch JMeter.
2. Add **Thread Group** by navigating to **Test Plan** | **Add** | **Threads(Users)** | **Thread Group**.
3. Add the **SOAP/XML-RPC Request** sampler to **Thread Group** by navigating to **Thread Group** | **Add** | **Sampler** | **SOAP/XML-RPC Request**.

4. Fill in the details of **SOAP/XML-RPC Request** as follows:

    ❏ **URL**: `http://wsf.cdyne.com/WeatherWS/Weather.asmx`

    ❏ **Send SOAPAction**: `http://ws.cdyne.com/WeatherWS/GetCityWeatherByZIP`

    ❏ **SOAP/XML-RPC Data**: This is given by the following code snippet:

```
<soapenv:Envelope xmlns:soapenv="http://schemas.xmlsoap.org/
soap/envelope/" xmlns:weat="http://ws.cdyne.com/WeatherWS/">
    <soapenv:Header/>
    <soapenv:Body>
        <weat:GetCityWeatherByZIP>
            <weat:ZIP>${__Random(20700,20900)}</weat:ZIP>
        </weat:GetCityWeatherByZIP>
    </soapenv:Body>
</soapenv:Envelope>
```

 Make sure the checkbox for **Send SOAPAction** is checked.

5. Add the **HTTP Request** component to **Thread Group** by navigating to **Thread Group | Add | Sampler | HTTP Request**.

6. Fill out the details of **HTTP Request** as follows:

    ❏ **Server Name or IP**: `wsf.cdyne.com`

    ❏ **Method**: `POST`

    ❏ **Path**: `/WeatherWS/Weather.asmx`

    ❏ **Body Data**: This is given by the following code snippet:

```
<soapenv:Envelope xmlns:soapenv="http://schemas.xmlsoap.org/
soap/envelope/" xmlns:weat="http://ws.cdyne.com/WeatherWS/">
    <soapenv:Header/>
    <soapenv:Body>
        <weat:GetCityWeatherByZIP>
            <weat:ZIP>${__
Random(20700,20900)}</weat:ZIP>
        </weat:GetCityWeatherByZIP>
    </soapenv:Body>
</soapenv:Envelope>
```

7. Add **HTTP Header Manager** as a child of **HTTP Request** by navigating to **HTTP Request | Add Config Element | HTTP Header Manager**.

8. Click on the **Add** button to add a header parameter.

9. Fill in the details as follows:

    ❑   **Name**: Content-Type

    ❑   **Value**: text/xml

10. Click on the **Add** button to add another header parameter. Fill in the following details:

    ❑   **Name**: SoapAction

    ❑   **Value**: http://ws.cdyne.com/WeatherWS/GetCityWeatherByZIP

11. Add the **View Results Tree** listener to your **Test Plan** by navigating to **Test Plan | Add | Listener | View Results Tree**.

12. Save and run the test plan. Observe the results of the execution as shown in the following screenshot:

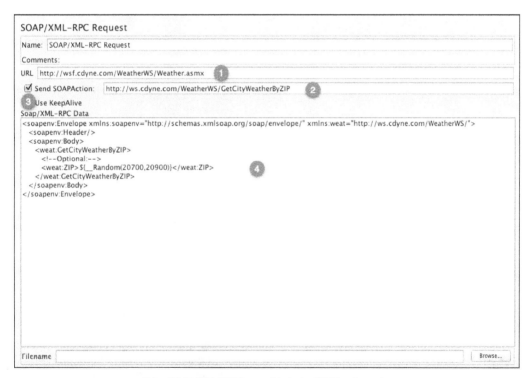

Using SOAP/XML-RPC Request to test a SOAP web service

The following screenshot shows an example of using the **HTTP Request** component to test SOAP web services:

HTTP Request

Name: HTTP Request

Comments:

Web Server | Timeouts (milliseconds)

Server Name or IP: wsf.cdyne.com ① | Port Number: | Connect: | Response:

HTTP Request

Implementation: | Protocol [http]: | Method: POST ② Content encoding:

Path: /WeatherWS/Weather.asmx ③

☐ Redirect Automatically ☑ Follow Redirects ☑ Use KeepAlive ☐ Use multipart/form-data for POST ☐ Browser-compatible headers

Parameters | Body Data

```
1  <soapenv:Envelope xmlns:soapenv="http://schemas.xmlsoap.org/soap/envelope/" xmlns:weat="http://ws.cdyne.com/WeatherWS/">
2     <soapenv:Header/>
3     <soapenv:Body>
4        <weat:GetCityWeatherByZIP>
5           <!--Optional:-->
6           <weat:ZIP>${__Random(20700,20900)}</weat:ZIP>      ④
7        </weat:GetCityWeatherByZIP>
8     </soapenv:Body>
9  </soapenv:Envelope>
```

Send Files With the Request:

File Path: | Parameter Name: | MIME Type:

Add | Browse... | Delete

Proxy Server

Server Name or IP: | Port Number: | Username | Password

Using HTTP Request to test a SOAP web service

How it works...

In this example, we are testing a weather service at `http://wsf.cdyne.com/WeatherWS/Weather.asmx`, which has been exposed as a SOAP web service. Our goal was to get the weather information for various ZIP or postal codes at the time we run our tests. To do that, we started out by creating a new test plan and adding **Thread Group** to it. In step 3, we added a **SOAP/XML-RPC Request** component to our test plan and filled it out with the appropriate details needed to satisfy our SOAP request. Such details include the URL where the service is housed, the SOAP action or operation that we intend to perform (`http://ws.cdyne.com/WeatherWS/GetCityWeatherByZIP` in our case), and the actual data in the form of XML we want to send. A sample of that data format can be seen at `http://wsf.cdyne.com/WeatherWS/Weather.asmx?op=GetCityForecastByZIP` or by examining the **web services definition language** (**WSDL**) file at `http://wsf.cdyne.com/WeatherWS/Weather.asmx?WSDL`. With all the details in, our **SOAP/XML-RPC** is ready to communicate with the service and retrieve weather information for any valid ZIP or postal code we supply. For the supplier ZIP code, on each invocation, we have used one of JMeter's built-in functions, `__Random()`, to randomize our ZIP code selection with a given boundary. `${__Random(20700,20900)}` will return random values within `20700` and `20900` for each invocation.

For illustrative purposes, we showed that the web service could also be tested with a **HTTP Request** component since it is communicating over HTTP. To do that, we added a **HTTP Request** component to **Thread Group** and configured it appropriately. This time, we set the server name to `wsf.cdyne.com` and the path to `/WeatherWS/Weather.asmx`. We changed the **HTTP Request** method to POST and sent the raw XML data through the body data of the request. With that configuration, the **HTTP Request** component mirrored the settings we configured for the **SOAP/XML-RPC** component, and can now also talk to the web service.

When we saved and ran the test plan, we observed that both components are able to communicate with the web service and report the server response.

 When you examine **Response Data** in the **View Results Tree** listener, responses from both **HTTP Request** and **SOAP/XML-RPC** might not give the same response as they might get supplied different ZIP codes at runtime.

The following screenshot demonstrates **View Results Tree**:

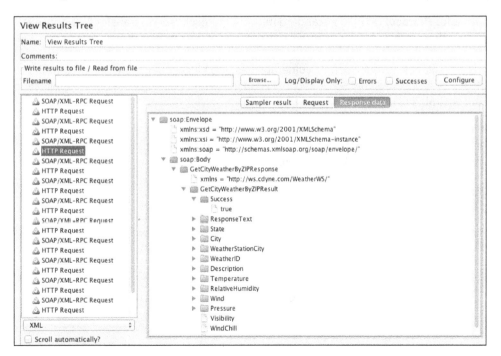

There's more...

SOAP web services are broader than we can cover in a single recipe, or even the entire book for that matter. For example, one of the main features of web services is that they can be securely protected, thus allowing only authorized consumers to invoke them. In most cases, authentication information can be passed with requests through the SOAP header attributes in SOAP messages for example. We strongly encourage you to read more content online. Super intrigued readers could also pick up books and resources on web services for an in-depth understanding of what is happening under the hood.

Another good resource for testing and understanding SOAP web services is SOAP UI, a freely available tool. It can be download from `http://www.soapui.org/`.

SOAP UI offers tons of features including generating sample requests for each operation exposed by a web service, security testing, intuitive GUI, and lots more. We encourage you to download a copy and evaluate it if you are primarily tasked with SOAP web services.

See also

Interested readers can read more on SOAP at `http://en.wikipedia.org/wiki/SOAP`.

Testing FTP services

File Transfer Protocol (**FTP**) is a standard network protocol used to transfer files between hosts over the Internet. Applications will normally use it as a means of uploading or downloading files to/from different hosts. FTP was not designed as a secure protocol, and as a result has several security vulnerabilities, the biggest being unencrypted traffic, which allows eavesdropping. Since security is an important aspect of almost all applications, it is not desirable to use FTP in its standard form.

SFTP is secure FTP, allowing all FTP communication to be secure over **Secure Shell** (**SSH**). In this form, all communication and data is encrypted, preventing preying eyes from intercepting communication and eavesdropping.

How to do it...

Out of the box, JMeter supports testing FTP. However, in this recipe, we will focus on testing SFTP, since as explained earlier, it is the most often encountered case due to its high security.

 This recipe relies on extending JMeter with a plugin.

Perform the following steps:

1. Install the JMeter SSH Sampler plugin:

   ❑ Download the JMeter plugin from `https://github.com/yciabaud/jmeter-ssh-sampler/releases`

   ❑ Download the JSCH JAR file from `http://devbucket-afriq.s3.amazonaws.com/jmeter-cookbook/jsch-0.1.51.jar`

   ❑ Copy the `ApacheJMeter_ssh-1.1.0.jar` file to the `$JMETER_HOME/lib/ext` directory

   ❑ Copy the `jsch-0.1.51.jar` file to the `$JMETER_HOME/lib` directory

2. Launch JMeter.

3. Add **Thread Group** by navigating to **Test Plan | Add | Threads(Users) | Thread Group**.

4. Add the **SSH SFTP** component to **Thread Group** by navigating to **Thread Group | Add | Sampler | SSH SFTP**.

5. Fill out the following details:

   ❑ **Hostname**: `${host}`

   ❑ **User Name**: `${user}`

   ❑ **Password**: `${password}`

   ❑ **Action**: `put`

   ❑ **Source path**: `${src}`

   ❑ **Destination path**: `${dest}`

6. Add two **CSV Data Set Config** elements by navigating to **Thread Group | Add | Config Element | CSV Data Set Config**.

7. Fill in the following parameter (leave everything else as it is):

   ❑ **Filename**: `sftp.txt`

8. Fill in the following parameter (leave everything else as it is):

   ❑ **Filename**: `sftp-files.txt`

9. Add the **View Results Tree** listener to your test plan by navigating to **Test Plan | Add | Listener | View Results Tree**.

10. Save the test plan.

11. Create two files (one named `sftp.txt` and a second named `sftp-files.txt`) in the same directory where the script resides.

12. The contents of the `sftp.txt` file should look similar to this:

```
host,user,password
your-host-ip,your-username,your-password
```

 This is provided just for illustrative purposes of what the structure of the file should look like. You should replace this with your own host, user, and password respectively!

13. The contents of the `sftp-files.txt` file should look similar to this:

```
src,dest
/tmp/a.txt,/tmp/output-a.txt
/tmp/b.txt,/tmp/output-b.txt
/tmp/c.txt,/tmp/output-c.txt
```

14. Save and run the test plan. Observe the results of the execution.

Confirm the files were successfully transferred by logging in to the SFTP server and verifying the files in the destination directory. Refer to the following screenshot for more details:

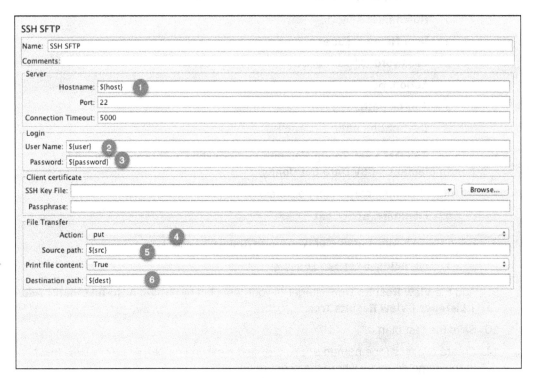

Configuring the SSH SFTP component

Alternatively, you could run a local FTP server on your machine to follow along with the example.

For Windows: `http://www.coreftp.com/server/`.

For Mac OS X: `http://igerry.com/desktop/apple-os/enabling-ftp-server-os-x-mavericks.html`.

For Unix: `http://www.sysadminshare.com/2011/03/enable-ftp-service-in-unix-server.html`.

To confirm that the files were securely transferred to the server, open a terminal window, log in, and list the contents of the target directory like we do in the following code snippet:

```
root@test:/tmp# ls -l
total 12
-rw-r--r-- 1 root root 149 May 11 22:48 output-a.txt
-rw-r--r-- 1 root root 149 May 11 22:48 output-b.txt
-rw-r--r-- 1 root root 149 May 11 22:48 output-c.txt
```

Refer to the following screenshot for more details:

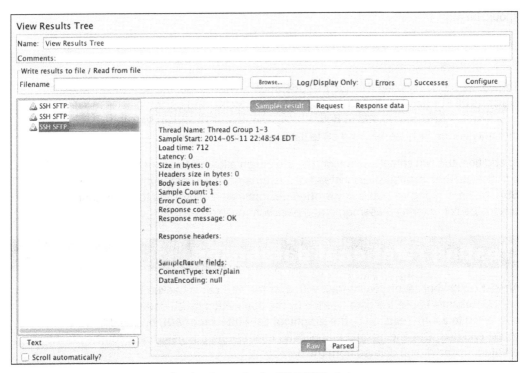

Results of executing the SSH SFTP test plan

How it works...

We started out by extending JMeter with the SSH Sampler plugin. This plugin provided SSH and SFTP features by adding two additional samplers (SSH Command and SSH SFTP) to JMeter's built-in samplers. One of these samplers, SSH SFTP, is just what we need to secure FTP connections to transfer files between hosts. As usual, we created a test plan, added **Thread Group** to it, and then added the SSH SFTP sampler as a child of **Thread Group**. Once added, we configured the SSH SFTP component with the details needed to communicate with our SFTP server. These included specifying a host, username, password, and operation to perform as well as the source and destination directories. In our case, since our goal is to transfer files from our local machine (or wherever the script is being run) to our SFTP server, we used a PUT action, which is the FTP action to put/store a local file you can't store to a remote location.

In addition, to make our scripts more robust, we added a CSV Data Set Config element to **Thread Group** to externalize these parameters from our scripts and supply them at runtime. This allows us to change the values without needing to change the script.

With all the relevant information configured, we were able to successfully transfer a couple of files from our local machine to the SFTP server as observed in the results listener. We also confirmed this by logging in to our SFTP server and verifying the files are at the location they should be at.

There's more...

Though we have only used a single FTP operation in this recipe, the SSH SFTP sampler supports all FTP actions. These include GET, RM, RMDIR, and LS. We use GET to download files from the SFTP server, RM to delete a file from the SFTP server, RMDIR to delete an entire directory on the SFTP server, and LS to list the contents of a directory on the SFTP server.

In addition, the two samplers provided by the plugin allow us to connect with the SSH client certificates, that is, public keys instead of a username/password combo. When working with SSH, authenticating via public key is often desirable as it allows you to easily connect to the box instead of entering a username and password each time.

Testing relational databases

Almost every application you interact with over the Internet is backed by a database of some sort. Databases house the data needed by the application. Such data is then retrieved and converted to a form required by the **graphical user interface** (**GUI**) by a middleware to display to the end user. Depending on the application needs and business logic, some data may be created, updated, and deleted from the database.

Sometimes, it is necessary to directly test databases outside the application(s) that use it. This may help identify database bottlenecks such as expensive table joins, missing table indexes, slow running queries, and so on.

How to do it...

In this recipe, we will cover how JMeter can be used to test a relational database directly. Perform the following steps:

 This recipe requires the use of a relational database, so we will set one up here. However, this will most likely have been set up for you, but we do this for illustrative purposes.

1. Set up an H2 database:
    - Download an H2 database distribution from `http://www.h2database.com/html/download.html`.
    - Extract the archive to a location of your choice. We will refer to this as `H2_HOME`.
    - From the command line, go to the `H2_HOME/bin` folder.
    - Start the H2 database server by issuing either of these commands:

      On Unix: `./h2.sh`

      On Windows: `h2.bat`

2. This will launch your browser and point to the H2 Admin console as shown in the upcoming screenshot.

3. Create a test database named `test` by changing your **JDBC URL** value to either of the following:
    - On Unix: `jdbc:h2:tcp://localhost//tmp/test;MVCC=TRUE`
    - On Windows: `jdbc:h2:tcp://localhost/c:/test;MVCC=TRUE`

4. Click on the **Connect** button.

5. Copy the contents of the `ch4.sql` script into the space provided in the console.

6. Click on the **Run** button.

7. This will create some tables and populate sample data for us to test with.

8. Now that we have a database and a table to test with, we can go ahead and configure a **JDBC Connection Configuration** component to point to it. Refer the following screenshot:

Since H2 is Java-based, to run it, you need to have a **Java Runtime Environment** (**JRE**) set up on the machine you are using. Please refer to *Appendix, Installing the Supporting Software Needed for this Book* for instructions on setting up a JRE on your machine if you don't already have one.

9. Copy the JDBC driver (`h2-1.4.178.jar` or similar) from the `H2_HOME/bin` folder to the `JMETER_HOME/lib` folder.

10. Add the **JDBC Connection Configuration** component to the test plan by right-clicking on **Test Plan** and navigating to **Test Plan | Add | Config Element | JDBC Connection Configuration**.

11. Configure the properties as follows:
    - **Variable Name**: `mydb`
    - **Validation Query**: `Select 1 from dual`
    - **Database URL**: `jdbc:h2:tcp://localhost//tmp/test;MVCC=TRUE` (those using Windows should use `jdbc:h2:tcp://localhost/c:/test;MVCC=TRUE`)
    - **JDBC Driver class**: `org.h2.Driver`
    - **Username**: `sa`

12. Leave the rest of the configurations as is.

13. Add **Thread Group** by navigating to **Test Plan | Add | Threads(User) | Thread Group**.

14. Add the **JDBC Request** sampler to **Thread Group** by navigating to **Thread Group | Add | Sampler | JDBC Request**.

15. Fill in the following details:

   ❑ **Variable Name**: `mydb` (should match the variable name specified in step 3)

   ❑ SQL Query: This is given by the following code snippet:

```
select *
from emp e
inner join dept d on d.deptno = e.deptno
```

16. Add the **View Results Tree** listener by navigating to **Thread Group | Add | Listener | View Results Tree**.

17. Add the **Aggregate Report** listener to **Thread Group | Add | Listener | Aggregate Report**.

18. Save and run the test plan. Observe the results.

How it works...

To test a relational database, JMeter offers two components, JDBC Connection Configuration and JDBC Request, both of which work in combination to make testing possible. The JDBC Connection Configuration component is needed to set up the connection to the database. The most important elements in its configuration are the database URL, JDBC driver class, the username, and the password. This information is needed to successfully connect to any relational database. In our case, we used H2 (a pure Java SQL database), but any other database such as Oracle, MySQL, Postgres, DB2, and so on will equally do. The way we are able to connect to any of these relational databases is through their JDBC driver classes, which come bundled in the form of a JAR file. The JAR file containing the driver class for your target database can be downloaded by searching online or at the vendor's website.

 You must copy this JDBC driver JAR to the `$JMETER_HOME/lib` directory and restart JMeter to make it available to your test plans.

Once the connection has been set up, to issue queries and requests to the database, we need the JDBC Request component. We added this to our **Thread Group**, and in our case, issued a query to list all employees, their department, and other relevant details such as hire date, compensation, and so on. If this query was used within an application, then it becomes important to know how fast the query is. To test its execution speed, we added an **Aggregate Report** listener to our test plan and increased the size of **Thread Group/users** to `100` with a loop of `3`. Once executed, in our case, we found the query performed quite well with a speed of about 3 milliseconds. With that in mind, if we used this in the context of an application and that application module is running slowly, say 12 seconds, then we could be certain that it wasn't the query running slow but rather some other parts of the module, and divert our attention to those.

There's more...

In our case, we issued a **SELECT** request to our database, but the JDBC Request component supports all other DDL operations including **INSERT**, **DELETE**, and **UPDATE**. In addition, it supports callable statements (used to execute stored procedures) and prepared statements (used to supply bind parameters and prevent SQL injection attacks).

Also, the JDBC Connection Configuration element allows you to supply the maximum number of connections. This can be configured to match what is configured on the application server settings to realistically mimic available connection settings to the application. Also, the JDBC Connection Configuration element allows you to choose the transaction isolation level for operations. It's best to leave it as **DEFAULT**, but other options are available as well should you need fine-grained control over transaction isolation levels.

Testing NoSQL databases

A new wave of databases categorized as NoSQL (Not Only SQL or No SQL depending on which interpretation you prefer) have burst on to the scene and offer some features not provided by relational databases that many applications have found invaluable and essential. Such features include document-oriented storage, the schema-less nature of documents, replication, high availability, sharding, map/reduce, and so on. Each of these bring something new to the table and allow applications to relay information and offer certain features they haven't been able to do with relational databases. Popular NoSQL databases include MongoDB, Couchbase, Redis, Apache Cassandra, Riak, and so on.

As such, it is not uncommon to encounter applications today entirely or partly backed by NoSQL databases. In fact, several of the applications we have used during the course of this book are backed up by NoSQL databases.

How to do it...

JMeter offers a way to directly test MongoDB (one of the most popular NoSQL databases) out of the box. In this recipe, we will see how to do just that. Perform the following steps:

1. Install MongoDB as described in
   `http://docs.mongodb.org/manual/installation/`.

    For easier use, make sure MONGODB_HOME/bin is available at your path, so you can access commands such as mongod and mongo easily from any terminal and/or directory.

2. Start the MongoDB instance with mongod.

3. Test that the connection is up and running by opening a terminal window and typing `mongo`. You should see a message similar to this on your terminal window:

```
MongoDB shell version: 2.6.1
connecting to: test
Server has startup warnings:
2014-05-13T19:58:11.240-0400 [initandlisten]
2014-05-13T19:58:11.240-0400 [initandlisten] ** WARNING: soft
rlimits too low. Number of files is 256, should be at least 1000
```

4. Launch JMeter.

5. Add **Thread Group** by navigating to **Test Plan | Add | Threads(Users) | Thread Group**.

6. Add the **MongoDB Source Config** element by navigating to **Thread Group | Add | Config Element | MongoDB Source Config**.

7. Fill in the contents as follows:

    ❑ **Server Address List**: 127.0.0.1

    ❑ **MongoDB Source**: mongo

 You can use any name you wish for the MongoDB source, but make sure it is unique if you have more than one MongoDB source configuration component.

8. Add the **MongoDB Script** component to **Thread Group** by navigating to **Thread Group | Add | Sampler | MongoDB Script**.

9. Fill in the following details:

    ❑ **MongoDB Source**: mongo (should match the name you specified in step 7)

    ❑ **Database Name**: jmeterDB

    ❑ **Username**: (leave it blank)

    ❑ **Password**: (leave it blank)

    ❑ **The script to run**: This is shown by the following code snippet:

```
db.jmeter.insert({"title":"This is it", "content": "Super
cool stuff", "comments": [{"user": "john doe", "comment": "I
didn't find this very useful."}, {"user": "lisa", "comment":
"Get a life!"}]});
db.jmeter.insert({"title":"Another Post", "content": "Super
cool stuff", "comments": [{"user": "john doe", "comment": "I
didn't find this very useful."}, {"user": "joan", "comment":
"Get a life!"}, {"user": "badboy", "comment": "This is all
very exciting."}]});
db.jmeter.insert({"title":"Working with JMeter", "content":
"Super cool stuff", "comments": [{"user": "cynthia",
```

```
                "comment": "Testing out comments."}]});
        db.jmeter.insert({"title":"Can Gatling overtake JMeter?",
        "content": "Gatling promises to deliver some cool stuff.
        JMeter still and ever will rule", "comments": []});
        db.jmeter.insert({"title":"Cloud Testing", "content": "Super
        cool stuff", "comments": [{"user": "mia", "comment": "I
        never knew you could do that!"}]});
        db.jmeter.insert({"title":"Bring Back Our girls", "content":
        "In Nigeria, a terrorist group called Boko Haram have
        taken hold of over 300 school girls", "comments": [{"user":
        "dele", "comment": "This is depressing.I didn't find this
        very useful."}, {"user": "kunle", "comment": "I pray for
        their safe return"}]});
```

> Any valid `mongo` script can be filled in by the `mongo-data.json` script to run text area depending on your testing needs. Here, we are just testing inserts. The script we run is bundled with the sample code under the name `mongo-data.json`.

10. Add the **View Results Tree** listener to **Test Plan** by navigating to **Test Plan | Add | Listener | View Results Tree**.

11. Save and run the test plan. Observe the results of the execution.

How it works...

To directly test a MongoDB database, JMeter comes bundled with two components, MongoDB Source Config and MongoDB Script. The former lets your specify connection details and options including write concern details. The latter lets you specify the database to use for operations, the username and password if any, and the actual script to run during test execution. In our previous example, we configured both and were able to successfully populate our target collection (JMeter) with some sample data.

The contents of our database can be seen by opening up a terminal, connecting to the `mongo` instance, selecting our target database, and issuing a query against the collection:

```
mongo
use jmeterDB
db.jmeter.find();
```

There's more...

Though we have chosen to run inserts in our example, any valid MongoDB operations can be run. These include `find()`, `update()`, `exists()`, `remove()`, and so on. A list of operations can be found on the MongoDB website at `http://docs.mongodb.org/manual/`, with a SQL comparison at `http://docs.mongodb.org/manual/reference/sql-comparison/`.

For those who are not fond of working on the terminal, there is **Robomongo**, a GUI tool to make working with MongoDB a little easier. It can be downloaded from `http://robomongo.org/`.

Testing JMS services

Another common service often found in some applications are **Java Message Service** (**JMS**) services. JMS services are message services that allow applications that run on the JVM to communicate with each other through message passing. There are two main channels of communication: Topics (pub/sub) or Queues (p2p). With Topics, a producer sends a message to a destination and all subscribers to that channel get the message. You can think of this as a mailing list. When you are subscribed or opt in for mails from a vendor, then you are added to their e-mail or mail distribution, and you receive all communication sent by the vendor afterwards. What subscribers choose to do with the received message is entirely up to them. With Queues, the producer sends a message to a destination and only one subscriber gets to pick up the message at a time. A classic use of a Queue for example could be sending out a registration mail to a new registrant of a website or sending a payment invoice for purchased items.

How to do it...

JMeter supports testing both Topics and Queues directly. In this recipe, we will focus on testing a Topic, but testing Queues follows a similar pattern. Perform the following steps:

 For this recipe, we will use a free and open source messaging server known as ActiveMQ. You can learn more about Apache ActiveMQ from `http://activemq.apache.org/`.

1. Download Apache ActiveMQ from `http://activemq.apache.org/download.html`. At the time of writing this, the latest release was version 5.9.1, which is what we will use.

2. Extract it to the location of your chosen directory. We will refer to this location as `ACTIVEMQ_HOME`.

3. Copy `activemq-all-<version>.jar` (`activemq-all-5.9.1.jar` In our case) from `$ACTIVEMQ_HOME` to the `$JMETER_HOME/lib` directory.

4. Open a terminal window, go to the `$ACTIVEMQ_HOME/bin` directory, and start `activemq`. Fill in the following details:
   - **On Unix**: `./activemq console`
   - **On Windows**: `activemq.bat console`

5. You should see logs similar to the following code:

```
INFO: Using default configuration
(you can configure options in one of these file: /etc/default/
activemq /Users/berinle/.activemqrc)
INFO: Invoke the following command to create a configuration file
./activemq setup [ /etc/default/activemq | /Users/berinle/.
activemqrc ]
INFO: Using java '/Library/Java/JavaVirtualMachines/jdk1.7.0_21.
jdk/Contents/Home/bin/java'
INFO: Starting in foreground, this is just for debugging purposes
(stop process by pressing CTRL+C)
Java Runtime: Oracle Corporation 1.7.0_21 /Library/Java/
JavaVirtualMachines/jdk1.7.0_21.jdk/Contents/Home/jre
...
INFO | Connector ws started
 INFO | Apache ActiveMQ 5.9.1 (localhost, ID:bayo-macbook.
local-50624-1400111865074-0:1) started
 INFO | For help or more information please see: http://activemq.
apache.org
```

6. Launch JMeter.

7. Add **Thread Group** by navigating to **Test Plan | Add | Threads(Users) | Thread Group**.

8. Add the **User Defined Variables** component by navigating to **Thread Group | Add | Config Element | User Defined Variables**.

9. Add the following variables to the **User Defined Variables** component:

Name	Value
contextFactory	org.apache.activemq.jndi.ActiveMQInitialContextFactory
providerUrl	tcp://localhost:61616
connectionFactory	ConnectionFactory
destination	dynamicTopics/jmeterTopic

10. Add the **JMS Publisher** component to **Thread Group** by navigating to **Thread Group | Add | Sampler | JMS Publisher**.

11. Fill in the following details:

   ❏ **Initial Context Factory**: ${contextFactory}

   ❏ **Provider URL**: ${providerUrl}

   ❏ **Connection Factory**: ${connectionFactory}

   ❏ **Destination**: ${destination}

   ❏ **Message source**: Select textarea radio button

- ❏ **Message Type**: `Select Text Message radio button`
- ❏ **Text Message or Object Message serialized to XML by XStream**: `test from jmeter`

12. Add **JMS Subscriber** to **Thread Group** by navigating to **Thread Group** | **Add** | **Sampler** | **JMS Subscriber**.

13. Fill in the following details:
    - ❏ **Initial Context Factory**: `${contextFactory}`
    - ❏ **Provider URL**: `${providerUrl}`
    - ❏ **Connection Factory**: `${connectionFactory}`
    - ❏ **Destination**: `${destination}`

14. Add the **View Results Tree** listener to your **Test Plan** by navigating to **Test Plan** | **Add** | **Listener** | **View Results Tree**.

15. Save and run the test plan. Observe the results of the execution.

How it works...

Our first step was to set up a messaging server to test with. Thankfully, Apache ActiveMQ is a free and open source messaging server that is super easy to set up. Once installed, we started the messaging server on a terminal window. To allow JMeter to communicate with the messaging server, we copied over the required JAR file to JMeter's `lib` directory. We then set up our test plan as usual, adding **Thread Group** and two JMS samplers, JMS Publisher and JMS Subscriber, needed to communicate with the messaging server. The former is responsible for producing or publishing messages, while the latter consumes the messages produced. To ensure that happens, we made sure both components were configured to read/write from the same `dynamicTopics/jmeterTopic` destination folder. We also took advantage of a neat feature of ActiveMQ here to dynamically create a destination for us (a Topic) on the fly. If not, we would have had to set up the Topic through an admin interface or similar to make the Topic available.

With all the configurations set up properly, we were able to run the test and observe our results that a message was in fact produced by the publisher and consumed by the subscriber just like we intended.

When the test is run, in the **View Results Tree** listener, you will notice a similar message on JMS Publisher:

```
Response code: 200
Response message: 1 messages published
```

The following message can be seen on JMS Subscriber:

```
Response code: 200
Response message: 1 message(s) received successfully
```

There's more...

JMS is a broad subject, and it's testing can't be fully covered in a few pages. In our previous sample, we elected text messages to directly enter into the space provided in the publisher component. JMS supports many more types of messages, including map, object, and bytes messages, each of which are supported by the component. Also, the component allows us to read messages from a file, or even pick up random files from a location. In addition, both the components support durability and selectors, two important features of JMS.

See also

There are several excellent resources on the Internet on JMS. For curious readers who want to explore more, some good starting resources are as follows:

- ▶ http://en.wikipedia.org/wiki/Java_Message_Service
- ▶ http://docs.oracle.com/javaee/6/tutorial/doc/bncdq.html

5
Diving into Distributed Testing

In this chapter, we will cover the following recipes:

- ▸ Testing applications with JMeter's master-slave setup
- ▸ Testing internal applications using JMeter and Vagrant
- ▸ Testing external facing applications using JMeter, Vagrant, and AWS
- ▸ Testing external facing applications using Flood.IO
- ▸ Testing external facing applications using BlazeMeter

Introduction

There are times when you will need to put more load on the applications under test. Such load may be more than a single machine can handle normally due to resource limitations such as RAM, CPU, and so on. As such, to get the target load on the application under test, you will need to distribute your tests across multiple machines. This is what is referred to as distributed testing.

Distributed testing is a form of testing that allows tests to be distributed across multiple machines on a network to achieve a target load while still keeping test results accurate. The results from each machine are then combined into a single result to give a final report as we would have had in the case of running on a single machine.

In this chapter, we will detail how to run tests across multiple machines. We will begin by seeing how to manually configure distributed testing in JMeter with a master-slave setup, and then see how to effortlessly automate the configuration of as many machines as needed to run our tests. In later recipes, we cover how to use some of the available Cloud services for testing and even see how to roll our own infrastructure in the Cloud when needed.

Testing applications with JMeter's master-slave setup

Out of the box, JMeter provides a way to perform distributed testing. This comes in the form of a master-slave setup. In this mode, there is a machine known as a master, which controls a number of client machines (JMeter instances) known as slaves. This approach has some benefits, including managing multiple JMeter instances remotely from the master node, automatically collecting test results from all slave nodes and aggregating them into a single report, and replicating test plans from the master node to slave nodes without the need to copy them to each server. That said, it also has some drawbacks, with the major one being the master quickly becoming a bottleneck as a result of collecting information from slaves in real time. In our experience, we have found this approach doesn't scale well if you have more than a couple of slave nodes. Refer to the other recipes in this chapter to see how to get past this hurdle.

How to do it...

Perform the following steps:

1. Install JMeter on machine 1. We will refer to this as `master`.
2. Install JMeter on machine 2. We will refer to this as `slave_one`.
3. Get the IP address of machine 2 on the network. Open a terminal window and run the following commands:
    - For Windows: `ipconfig`
    - For Unix/Mac OS: `ifconfig | grep inet`
4. Edit `JMETER_HOME/bin/jmeter-server`, uncomment the line starting with `#RMI_HOST_DEF`, and replace it with the IP address retrieved from step 2, for example, `RMI_HOST_DEF=-Djava.rmi.server.hostname= 172.28.128.3`.
5. Start the JMeter server script using the following instructions:
    - For Windows: `JMETER_HOME/bin/jmeter-server.bat`
    - For Unix/Mac OS: `JMETER_HOME/bin/jmeter-server`
6. On the master JMeter installation, edit `JMETER_HOME/bin/jmeter.properties` and add the IP address of the slave node. Look for the line starting with `remote_hosts=127.0.0.1` and replace `127.0.0.1` with the IP address of the slave node, for example, `remote_hosts= 172.28.128.3`.
7. Repeat steps 2 to 6 on machine 3, which we will refer to as `slave_two`.

When adding additional IPs to the `remote_hosts` property, be sure to separate them with a comma, for example, `remote_hosts=172.28.128.3,172.28.128.4`.

8. Launch the JMeter GUI on the master.

9. Open the `scripts/ch5/cloud/shoutbox_loop.jmx` test plan bundled with the book samples. Alternatively, it can be downloaded from `http://bit.ly/1rvb1bv`.

10. Execute the test on the slave nodes by navigating to **Run | Remote Start All**.

The following diagram illustrates the architecture of a master-slave setup:

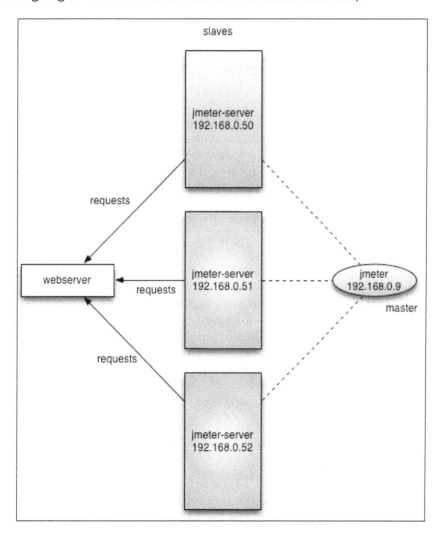

Since the script starts 200 users on each slave node and we run the test on both configured nodes, the following screenshot shows the test hitting the peak of 400 users:

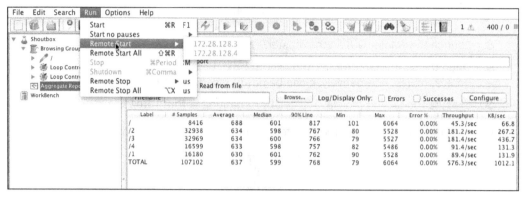

Controlling slave nodes via a JMeter master

How it works...

In a master-slave setup, the machines communicate over **remote method invocation** (**RMI**). On the slave nodes, we set up the communication by editing `RMI_HOST_DEF` in the `jmeter-server` file and then set up the master to be able to talk to each slave by adding the slave's IP address to the list of `remote_hostserver` in the `jmeter.properties` file. Once configured, we are able to start the test script loaded in the master node remotely on each slave mode, thereby distributing the load.

There's more...

As explained in the introduction of this recipe, this approach has its drawbacks. Thankfully, we are not limited to it as the only way to achieve distributed testing in JMeter. We can eliminate the master completely and eliminate any bottlenecks that arise from it, allowing us to scale a lot more as a result. Additionally, we can take advantage of Cloud providers offering distributed testing via JMeter and eliminate most mundane setup tasks. For this and much more, see the other recipes in this chapter.

See also

- ▶ http://jmeter.apache.org/usermanual/jmeter_distributed_testing_step_by_step.pdf
- ▶ http://en.wikipedia.org/wiki/Java_remote_method_invocation

Testing internal applications using JMeter and Vagrant

Until an application becomes external and public facing on the Internet for users to see, access to it remains internal to a company's network barricaded by firewalls. Only users on the company's intranet and network can get to the application. Due to this reason, testing such applications from external machines would be impossible unless some firewall rules are changed to allow it. Often, making such changes is time-consuming and sometimes not even allowed due to company policies. The next best thing is to configure the test servers within your company's network that can connect to the internal application under test, while still keeping the company's application private. This is a win-win situation and one you will normally encounter.

Configuring machines for testing from scratch can be a daunting task, especially when the same steps have to be repeated from one machine to the other. Performing such tasks manually becomes mundane and error prone. What if there was a way to write a script describing just how each machine should be set up, and we could run this script to automate the configuration of any machine for testing? Thankfully, there is!

Vagrant is a tool to create and configure lightweight, reproducible, and portable development environments. It allows us to automate machine creation and configuration, making what would have been a daunting and error prone process painless. More information about Vagrant can be found at `http://www.vagrantup.com/`.

> Vagrant and Virtualbox are cross-platform and work equally well on Windows and Unix operating systems alike.

How to do it...

In this recipe, we will cover how to distribute our test between two machines on a network. We will assume that the application we are testing is closed to the world and only visible from within our network. Perform the following steps:

1. Download and install Vagrant as described in the *Appendix, Installing Supporting Software Needed for the Book*.

2. Download and extract the bundled scripts accompanying the book (`82800S_ch5_recipe_vagrant_internal.zip`), or alternatively clone the GitHub repository at `https://github.com/jmeter-cookbook/recipe_vagrant_internal_shell` on each machine you want to use as a test server.

Vagrant requires VirtualBox or VMware Fusion to run. Make sure they are installed on each machine before proceeding. At the time of writing this book, Vagrant is at version 1.6.2 and VirtualBox at 4.3.12. These are the versions we use throughout the book. Refer to the *Appendix* for installation instructions.

3. On each machine, open a terminal window and change the directory of the extract (or GitHub clone) and run the following code:

```
vagrant up
```

4. You should see logs similar to the following code:

```
Bringing machine 'default' up with 'virtualbox' provider...
==> default: Clearing any previously set network interfaces...
==> default: Available bridged network interfaces:
1) en0: Ethernet
2) en1: Wi-Fi (AirPort)
    default: What interface should the network bridge to? 1
==> default: Preparing network interfaces based on
configuration...
    default: Adapter 1: nat
    default: Adapter 2: bridged
==> default: Forwarding ports...
    default: 1099 => 1097 (adapter 1)
    default: 22 => 2222 (adapter 1)
==> default: Booting VM...
==> default: Waiting for machine to boot. This may take a few
minutes...
...
```

5. Run `vagrant status` to verify whether a virtual machine has been set up and is running. You should see something similar to the following code:

```
Current machine states:
default                    running (virtualbox)
```

6. Connect to the virtual machine by running `vagrant ssh`.

7. On VirtualBox, ensure JMeter has been properly set up at `/usr/local/apache-jmeter-2.11` by running the following code:

```
/usr/local/apache-jmeter-2.11/bin/jmeter.sh -v
```

8. You should see logs similar to the following code:

```
…
Copyright (c) 1998-2014 The Apache Software Foundation
Version 2.11 r1554548
```

9. Repeat steps 5 to 7 on the other box(es) to ensure they are ready for testing.

10. Run the bundled test plan on each machine by running the following code:

```
/usr/local/apache-jmeter-2.11/bin/jmeter -n -t /vagrant/testplans/
shoutbox_loop.jmx -l /vagrant/testplans/output.csv
```

11. Wait until the test finishes executing on each box. You should see something similar to the following code:

```
2014/05/27 17:20:45 INFO  - jmeter.engine.StandardJMeterEngine:
Notifying test listeners of end of test
2014/05/27 17:20:45 INFO  - jmeter.reporters.Summariser: summary +
2711 in   17s =  160.7/s Avg:   521 Min:    76 Max:  1677 Err:
0 (0.00%) Active: 0 Started: 200 Finished: 200
summary +   2711 in   17s =  160.7/s Avg:   521 Min:    76 Max:
1677 Err:    0 (0.00%) Active: 0 Started: 200 Finished: 200
2014/05/27 17:20:45 INFO  - jmeter.reporters.Summariser: summary =
7800 in 45.4s =  171.7/s Avg:   470 Min:    76 Max:  6100 Err:
1 (0.01%)
summary =   7800 in  45.4s =  171.7/s Avg:   470 Min:    76 Max:
6100 Err:    1 (0.01%)
Tidying up ...    @ Tue May 27 17:20:45 UTC 2014 (1401211245810)
... end of run
```

12. Gather the results from each box by copying each output to a common accessible location on your network. In our case, the output file on each box is written to the `testplans` directory, which can be seen on the host machine.

 You can use a sync service like Dropbox (http://www.dropbox.com) to share files between two or more machines if you are having difficulty sharing files between your test servers.

13. Merge the output from all test boxes into one file. Readers following along on Windows can do that in a text editor. On Unix, we can use a `cat` command as follows:

```
cat output1.csv output2.csv >> merged-output.csv
```

14. Launch the JMeter GUI.

15. Add the **Summary Report** listener by navigating to **Test Plan | Add | Listener | Summary Report**.

16. Click on **Summary Report**.

17. Click on the **Browse...** button. Select the `merged-output.csv` file and observe the results of the test, as shown in the following screenshot:

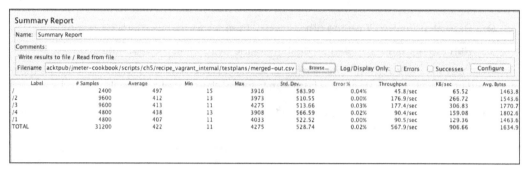

Summary Report of output on an internal virtual machine

How it works...

Our goal in this recipe was to distribute our test load between two machines on the network. We started out by installing Vagrant, a tool to help us build and configure machines with minimal fuss on each target machine. Using a configuration file (`Vagrantfile`), we were able to configure two machines with JMeter installed and ready to run our test scripts (steps 3 to 8). Once configured, we ran our tests in non-GUI mode, specifying additional commands when starting JMeter (step 10). The `-n` command instructed JMeter to run in non-GUI mode, `-t` told it what file to run, and `-l` specified the location to write the results of the test execution to.

Once each box completed its test, we gathered the results from each individual box and then merged the results into one. We were then able to view the combined results of the distributed load test with JMeter's **Summary Report** listener.

There's more...

Using the same concepts illustrated in this recipe, we can create many more virtual machines to meet the targeted load for testing. If the application is public facing, then we could gain access to many more machines through Cloud services and infrastructure to perform our tests. For more on leveraging the Cloud for distributed testing, see the following recipes:

▶ *Testing external facing applications using JMeter, Vagrant, and AWS*

▶ *Testing external facing applications using Flood.IO*

▶ *Testing external facing applications using BlazeMeter*

Testing external facing applications using JMeter, Vagrant, and AWS

Once the target test load of an application reaches a certain point (it varies from application to application), you can no longer accurately perform tests on it from a single box. The main reason for this is resource limitation. Each machine, no matter how powerful it is, is limited by RAM, processor speed, and so on. A clever workaround to resource limitation is divide-and-conquer. With this technique, the test load can be distributed to several low- or middle-end machines, thus achieving the target test goal without sacrificing test accuracy.

Amazon Web Services (**AWS**) offers a broad set of global compute, storage, database, analytics, application, and deployment services that help them move faster and scale applications with lower IT costs. With its services, we can create several virtual machines needed for our distributed load test without having to worry about all the low-level infrastructure details. More information about AWS can be found at `https://aws.amazon.com/`.

 To follow along with this recipe, you need an AWS account. You can register for free at `https://aws.amazon.com`.

How to do it...

In this recipe, we will see how we can leverage Vagrant and AWS to conduct distributed testing with JMeter, essentially rolling out our own testing infrastructure in the Cloud. Perform the following steps:

1. Download and install Vagrant by navigating to `http://www.vagrantup.com/`.

2. Open a terminal window and run the following command: `vagrant plugin install vagrant-aws`. You will see logs similar to the following code:

   ```
   Installing the 'vagrant-aws' plugin. This can take a few
   minutes...
   Building nokogiri using packaged libraries.
   ...
   Installed the plugin 'vagrant-aws (0.4.1)'!
   ```

3. Clone the project from GitHub at `https://github.com/jmeter-cookbook/recipe_vagrant_aws_shell` and follow the `README.md` instructions or download the recipe bundle with the book (`8280OS_ch5_recipe_vagrant_aws.zip`).

4. Modify the following entries in the `Vagrantfile` with the appropriate settings from your AWS account and save the file when done:

```
aws.access_key_id = "YOUR AWS KEY ID"
aws.secret_access_key = "YOUR AWS SECRET KEY"
aws.keypair_name = "YOUR KEYPAIR NAME"
aws.region = "YOUR AWS REGION"
override.ssh.private_key_path = "PATH TO YOUR PRIVATE KEY"
```

> Your access key, secret access key, and keypair can be obtained by following the documentation at http://aws.amazon.com/documentation/ec2/.

5. On the terminal, run `vagrant up vm1 --provider=aws` to create and start the first virtual machine. You should see logs similar to the following code:

```
Bringing machine 'vm1' up with 'aws' provider...
[fog] [WARNING] Unable to load the 'unf' gem. Your AWS strings may
not be properly encoded.
==> vm1: HandleBoxUrl middleware is deprecated. Use HandleBox
instead.
==> vm1: This is a bug with the provider. Please contact the
creator
==> vm1: of the provider you use to fix this.
==> vm1: Warning! The AWS provider doesn't support any of the
Vagrant
==> vm1: high-level network configurations (`config.vm.network`).
They
==> vm1: will be silently ignored.
==> vm1: Launching an instance with the following settings...
==> vm1:   -- Type: m1.small
==> vm1:   -- AMI: ami-7747d01e
==> vm1:   -- Region: us-east-1
==> vm1:   -- Keypair: cookbook-key
==> vm1:   -- Block Device Mapping: []
==> vm1:   -- Terminate On Shutdown: false
==> vm1:   -- Monitoring: false
==> vm1:   -- EBS optimized: false
==> vm1: Waiting for instance to become "ready"...
==> vm1: Waiting for SSH to become available...
==> vm1: Machine is booted and ready for use!
...
==> vm1: notice: /Stage[main]/Java::Package_debian/Package[java]/
ensure: ensure changed 'purged' to 'present'
==> vm1: notice: Finished catalog run in 111.06 seconds
```

6. Run `vagrant up vm2 --provider=aws` to create and start the second virtual machine.

7. Verify that both machines are running with the `vagrant status` command. You should see the following logs:

```
Current machine states:
vm1                     running (aws)
vm2                     running (aws)
```

8. Verify that both machines are ready for testing by running the following commands on both machines:

```
vagrant ssh vm1 (or vagrant ssh vm2 for the second machine)
/usr/local/apache-jmeter-2.11/bin/jmeter -v
```

9. Run the bundled test plan on each machine by running the following code:

```
/usr/local/apache-jmeter-2.11/bin/jmeter -n -t /vagrant/testplans/
shoutbox_loop.jmx -l /vagrant/testplans/output.csv
```

10. Wait until the test finishes executing on each box. You should see something similar to the following code:

```
...
2014/05/27 22:33:22 INFO  - jmeter.threads.JMeterThread: Thread
finished: Browsing Group 1-199
2014/05/27 22:33:22 INFO  - jmeter.threads.JMeterThread: Thread
finished: Browsing Group 1-196
2014/05/27 22:33:23 INFO  - jmeter.threads.JMeterThread: Thread
finished: Browsing Group 1-200
2014/05/27 22:33:23 INFO  - jmeter.engine.StandardJMeterEngine:
Notifying test listeners of end of test
2014/05/27 22:33:23 INFO  - jmeter.reporters.Summariser: summary +
6226 in    25s = 249.8/s Avg:    118 Min:    13 Max:  1757 Err:
0 (0.00%) Active: 0 Started: 200 Finished: 200
summary +   6226 in    25s =  249.8/s Avg:    118 Min:    13 Max:
1757 Err:     0 (0.00%) Active: 0 Started: 200 Finished: 200
2014/05/27 22:33:23 INFO  - jmeter.reporters.Summariser: summary =
7800 in  31.2s =  250.1/s Avg:    131 Min:    13 Max:  2069 Err:
0 (0.00%)
summary =    7800 in  31.2s =  250.1/s Avg:    131 Min:    13 Max:
2069 Err:     0 (0.00%)
Tidying up ...     @ Tue May 27 22:33:23 UTC 2014 (1401230003229)
... end of run
```

11. Gather the results from each box by copying each output to a commonly accessible location on your network using a command-line utility like `scp`. In our case, the output file on each box is written to the `testplans` directory on the virtual machine since that is the location we specified as the output directory. For example, we grabbed the files from our virtual machines using the following syntax:

```
scp -i [PATH TO YOUR KEYPAIR FILE] ubuntu@[HOST IP ]:/vagrant/
testplans/[OUTPUT FILE CSV] .
```

12. For example, look at the following code:

```
scp -i ~/cookbook-key.pem ubuntu@50.16.19.128:/vagrant/testplans/
output.csv vm1-out.csv
scp -i ~/cookbook-key.pem ubuntu@54.87.206.240:/vagrant/testplans/
output.csv vm2-out.csv
```

 You can also use a GUI tool such as **Cyberduck** (`http://cyberduck.io/`) to retrieve files from the virtual machine boxes if the command line isn't your cup of tea.

13. Merge the output from all test boxes into one file. Readers following along on Windows can do that in a text editor. On Unix, we can use a `cat` command as follows:

```
cat vm1-out.csv vm2-out.csv >> merged-output.csv
```

14. Launch the JMeter GUI.

15. Add the **Summary Report** listener by navigating to **Test plan | Add | Listener | Summary Report**.

16. Click on **Summary Report**.

17. Click on the **Browse...** button.

18. Select the `merged-output.csv` file and observe the results of the test.

19. Shut down the virtual machines by running `vagrant destroy`.

 AWS is a paid service, and you are charged by the hour per instance. Be sure to stop the instances when done with your tests to avoid unnecessary charges.

The **Summary Report** of our AWS test execution is shown in the following screenshot:

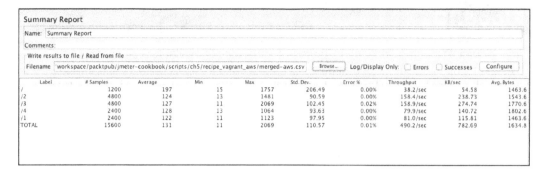

How it works...

Our goal in this recipe was to distribute our test load between two virtual machines in the Cloud. We started out by installing Vagrant, a tool to help us build and configure machines with minimal fuss on each target machine. Secondly, we installed the `vagrant-aws` plugin, which allows Vagrant to create, configure, and manage machines on an AWS infrastructure. Using a configuration file (`Vagrantfile`), we were able to configure two machines with JMeter installed and ready to run our test scripts. Once configured, we ran our tests in non-GUI mode specifying additional commands when starting JMeter (step 9). The `-n` command instructed JMeter to run in non-GUI mode, `-t` told it what file to run, and `-l` specified the location to write the results of the test execution to.

Once each box completed its test, we gathered the results from each individual box using the `scp` command (or any such similar tools) and then merged the results into one. We were then able to view the combined results of the distributed load test with JMeter's **Summary Report** listener.

There's more...

This recipe covered how to roll out our own testing Cloud infrastructure with ease. There are times when you will have a need to do this. One good reason could be lowering your company's IT cost as this route is far cheaper than maintaining the infrastructure yourself. Also, there are alternative Cloud services dedicated solely to testing purposes. See the following recipes for more information:

▶ The *Testing external facing applications using Flood.IO* recipe

▶ The *Testing external facing applications using BlazeMeter* recipe

Testing external facing applications using Flood.IO

When it comes to distributed testing, there is no shortage of available Cloud services that have sprung up in recent years that do an excellent job of minimizing the time it takes to set up and run tests. One such service is Flood.IO, located at https://flood.io. In their words, Flood.IO takes the pain out of setting up and maintaining a Cloud-based load and performance test infrastructure. By not having to set up and configure machines for testing, one huge task is taken off from our plates and we are able to focus on what we are really after, that is, testing our application. Beyond setup and configuration, this service provides beautiful and detailed analysis reports, real-time monitoring of test execution, the ability to scale globally on demand, and lots more.

At the time of writing this book, Flood.IO offers both free and paid services. The free service however is limited, as you might expect and only allows you to run tests for a maximum of 5 minutes. Since the node is shared, you might need to wait for it to become available if any other users are also using it at the same time.

How to do it...

In this recipe, we will show you how to use Flood.IO to run a distributed test plan in the Cloud. Since we will be using the free plan, the test is only run within a grid, but that is sufficient for our purposes.

 This recipe requires you to create a free account with Flood.IO.

1. Create a Flood.IO account at https://flood.io.
2. Log in to your account.
3. Click on the **Create Flood** button on the dashboard.
4. Under **Files**, upload the shoutbox_loop.jmx file bundled with the book (82800S_ch5_cloud_testing.zip). This is also available at https://github.com/jmeter-cookbook/cloud_testing/raw/master/shoutbox_loop.jmx.
5. Leave the enabled script validation on so that the script can be validated for correctness.
6. Under **Grids**, select a grid to run the test in. Since we are on a free account, only one grid will be available.
7. Fill in the following details for the rest of the variables on the **Create Flood** page:
   - **Name**: shoutbox loop
   - **Tags**: cookbook

- **Threads**: 1000
- **Rampup**: 90
- **Duration**: 600

8. Click on the **Start Flood** button.
9. Your test should begin shortly after (this may vary depending on the queue for the box) and start reporting live results from the test execution.
10. Wait for the test simulation to finish and observe the detailed reports.

 A link to the reports of the test simulation we ran for this recipe is located at https://flood.io/nffYmfOzfuGIFZyWtpN8LA.

The creation of floods is shown in the following screenshot:

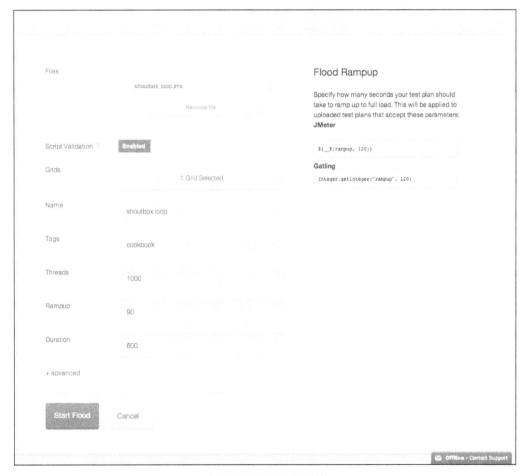

Files
shoutbox_loop.jmx
Remove file

Script Validation ? Enabled

Grids
1 Grid Selected

Name
shoutbox loop

Tags
cookbook

Threads
1000

Rampup
90

Duration
600

+ advanced

Start Flood   Cancel

Flood Rampup

Specify how many seconds your test plan should take to ramp up to full load. This will be applied to uploaded test plans that accept these parameters:
JMeter

${__P(rampup, 120)}

Gatling

Integer.getInteger("rampup", 120)

Offline - Contact Support

Creating a flood in Flood.IO

How it works...

Getting our test simulations running in the Cloud was as easy as it can be. All we need to do is create an account with Flood.IO and then proceed to create a test simulation, which in their terms is referred to as a flood. We then uploaded a prerecorded test plan from our local machine to their service and chose to run in the free available grid. Though optional, we specified the name for our flood and gave it a tag. Since our uploaded test simulation uses JMeter's property function, that is, `${__P(threads, 200)}`, and `${__P(rampup, 30)}` to specify the number of threads to run and how quickly those should be ramped up, we specified `1000` and `90` to override the defaults. This allowed us to simulate up to 1000 users ramped up over a 90-second period. We also elected to run our test for `10` minutes by specifying a duration of `600` in the **Duration** box.

 The free tier account only allows you to run the test for 5 minutes at a time before prematurely stopping your tests.

Once the flood is started, we are immediately transitioned into a live reporting view to show real-time analysis of the test simulation, as seen in the following screenshot:

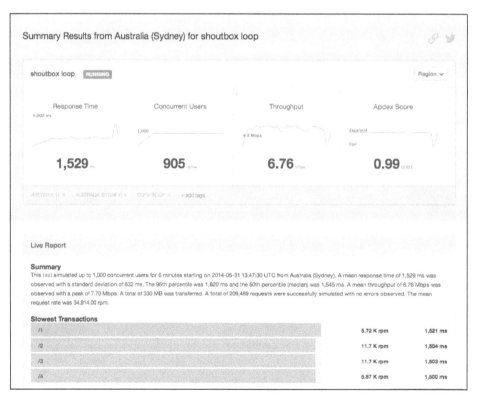

Live reporting of a test simulation run on Flood.IO

These reports are detailed and we can trace each individual transaction by clicking on them for even further analysis.

There's more...

The paid plans allow you to run tests for longer and even customize grids to your liking. Through the `ruby-jmeter` gem covered in the *Writing Test scripts through Ruby DSL* recipe in *Chapter 8, Beyond the Basics* we can run our test plans developed in Ruby right in the Cloud without even visiting the web UI. All that is needed is our Flood.IO API token, which can be retrieved under the security section of your account settings.

So, as an example, using the `ruby-jmeter` gem, we can replicate our recipe completely from the comfort of our local box without needing to fiddle with the UI at all. The code sample is located at xxx and is also bundled with the code bundle of this book.

Assuming you have installed the `ruby-jmeter` gem, registered an account with Flood. IO, and retrieved your API token key, you can save the following contents to a Ruby file, say `shoutbox_loop.rb` (located at `https://github.com/jmeter-cookbook/cloud_testing`), and run your simulation in the Cloud. Once saved, you can type `ruby shoutbox_loop.rb` to run. This is shown in the following code snippet:

```ruby
require 'rubygems'
require 'ruby-jmeter'
test do
  cookies clear_each_iteration: false
  threads count: 1000, rampup: 90, duration: (60 * 5), continue_
forever: true do
    defaults :domain => 'evening-citadel-2263.herokuapp.com'
    random_timer 1000, 2000
    visit name: 'Home', url: '/'
    visit name: 'Page 2', url: '/2'
    visit name: 'Page 3', url: '/3'
    visit name: 'Page 4', url: '/4'
    visit name: 'Page 3', url: '/3'
    visit name: 'Page 2', url: '/2'
    visit name: 'Home', url: '/'
  end
end.flood('API TOKEN KEY')
```

Once you hit *Enter*, the gem responds with a URL to the results of your test, which you can then open in your browser to see live results like we did earlier.

The results for our simulation run are located at:
`https://flood.io/4ddgffykQBuMBDQR8sSOnA.`

See also

> ▸ The *Writing Test scripts through Ruby DSL* recipe in *Chapter 8, Beyond the Basics*
>
> ▸ The *Testing external facing applications using BlazeMeter* recipe
>
> ▸ `https://github.com/flood-io/ruby-jmeter#running-a-jmeter-test-plan-on-floodio`

Testing external facing applications using BlazeMeter

Another Cloud service we could use for distributed testing is BlazeMeter, located at `http://blazemeter.com/`. In their words, BlazeMeter offers you your own elastic performance testing Cloud. By not having to set up and configure machines for testing, one huge task is taken off from our plates and we are able to focus on what we are really after, testing our application.

At the time of this writing, BlazeMeter offers both free and paid services. The free service however is limited, as you might expect, and only allows you to run a maximum of 50 concurrent users on shared servers with reports retained for only 24 hours. This is enough to illustrate the concept in this recipe, so that is what we will be using.

How to do it...

In this recipe, we will show you how to use BlazeMeter to run a distributed test plan in the Cloud. Since we will be using the free plan, we are limited to a maximum of 50 concurrent users on a shared machine.

 This recipe requires you to create a free account with BlazeMeter.

1. Create a BlazeMeter account at `http://blazemeter.com/`.
2. Log in to your account.
3. Click on the **+** button on the top navigation bar.
4. In the **Text Name** box, enter `shoutbox loop`.
5. Leave the default load origin as `-is`.
6. Click on the **Upload Files** button and upload the `shoutbox_loop.jmx` file bundled with the book. This is also available at `https://github.com/jmeter-cookbook/cloud_testing/raw/master/shoutbox_loop.jmx`.

7. Change the **Rampup** setting to 10 seconds by dragging on the corresponding slider.

8. Change the **Duration** setting to 10 minutes by dragging on the corresponding slider.

9. Change the JMeter version to **2.11**.

10. Leave the rest of the attributes at their default state.

11. Click on the **Save** button to save the test.

12. Click on the **Start** button to begin the test run.

13. Your test should begin shortly after (this may vary depending on the queue for the box) and start reporting live results from the test execution.

14. Wait for the test simulation to finish and observe the detailed reports. This is demonstrated in the following screenshot:

Adding a new test in BlazeMeter

How it works...

Getting our test simulations running in the Cloud is easy. All we need to do is create an account with BlazeMeter and then proceed to create a test simulation. We then uploaded a prerecorded test plan from our local machine to their service and chose to run on the freely shared server. We changed the ramp up setting to `10` seconds and duration to `10` minutes respectively. With those settings, we saved our test simulation and clicked on the **Start** button to begin the simulation run.

 The free tier account only allows you to run tests for a maximum of 1 hour with 50 concurrent users.

Once the test simulation is started, we can view live results by switching to the reports view. Once the test finishes, an e-mail is sent to you with a link to the detailed report of the simulation run. The report includes various tabs to help give a different perspective of the test run. You are able to track individual transactions, errors, hits/sec, CPU, network I/O, and so on. You can view the reports for our own test run at `https://a.blazemeter.com/report/NTgyOTE1`.

There's more...

The paid plans allow you to run tests for longer and spin off a lot more load. Whatever you use, you can be assured BlazeMeter has a plan to accommodate you. In addition, BlazeMeter provides a Chrome browser extension to help ease recording test plans and help run the recorded test plan directly in the Cloud on their infrastructure.

See also

▶ The *Testing external facing applications using JMeter, Vagrant, and AWS* recipe

▶ The *Testing external facing applications using Flood.IO* recipe

▶ The *Recording scripts via the Chrome browser extension* recipe in *Chapter 1, JMeter Fundamentals*

6
Extending JMeter

In this chapter, we will cover the following recipes:

- ▸ Using REST Sampler
- ▸ Using Ultimate Thread Group
- ▸ Using Throughput Shaping Timer
- ▸ Using Console Status Logger
- ▸ Using Dummy Sampler
- ▸ Developing custom JMeter plugins
- ▸ Testing WebSocket-enabled applications

Introduction

No matter how good a tool is, it normally won't provide all the user needs out of the box. As such, it is important to provide a means by which the tool can be extended to provide additional functionality. Such extensions can turn an already good tool into a great one.

JMeter is no different. It provides extension points in the form of plugins. Since JMeter is written in Java, plugins are nothing more than compiled byte code packaged as **Java Archives (JARs)**.

In this chapter, we will detail how to extend JMeter's functionality by installing some excellent and well-thought-out plugins, and dive into the details of how to use some of the components they provide. In the last recipe, we teach you how to write a custom JMeter plugin from scratch.

Using REST Sampler

As we explained in *Chapter 4, Testing Services,* **Representational State Transfer** (**REST**) is an architecture style of designing networked applications that relies on stateless, client-server, cacheable communications protocol (HTTP). It is lightweight and easily testable mainly because all communications between client and server are over HTTP.

More information about REST can be found at `http://en.wikipedia.org/wiki/Representational_state_transfer`.

How to do it...

In this recipe, we will cover how to test REST web services with the REST Sampler extension. The main feature of this extension is to allow us to interact with services that work only on XML. As such, it allows us to deal with XML payloads easily.

 REST Sampler can also be used with a service that consumes and produces JSON.

1. Download the `Extras with Libs` set of plugins from `http://jmeter-plugins.org/`.

2. Install the plugins by doing the following:

    1. Extract the ZIP archive to the location of your choice.

    2. Copy the `ExtrasLibs.jar` JMeter plugins from the `ext` directory of the extracted location to `$JMETER_HOME/lib/ext directory`.

    3. Copy all the JAR files from the `lib` directory of the extracted location to the `$JMETER_HOME/lib` directory.

3. Launch JMeter.

4. Add **Thread Group** by navigating to **Test Plan | Add | Threads(Users) | Thread Group**.

5. Add the **User Defined Variable** component by navigating to **Thread Group | Add | Config Element | User Defined Variable**.

6. Click on the **Add** button to add the following variables:

   ❑ **Name**: `base_url`

   ❑ **Value**: `http://api-jcb.herokuapp.com`

7. Add the **HTTP Header Manager** component to **Thread Group** by navigating to **Thread Group | Add | Config Element | HTTP Header Manager**.

8. Click on the **Add** button to add a header attribute with the following parameters:

   ❑ **Name**: `Content-Type`

   ❑ **Value**: `application/xml`

9. Click on the **Add** button again to add a second header attribute with the following parameters:

   ❑ **Name**: `Accept`

   ❑ **Value**: `application/xml`

10. Add **REST Sampler** to **Thread Group** by navigating to **Thread Group | Add | Sampler | jp@gc – REST Sampler**.

11. Fill in the details for **REST Sampler** as follows:

    ❑ **Name**: `Create Holiday Request`

    ❑ **Method**: `POST`

    ❑ **Base Url**: `${base_url}`

    ❑ **Port**: `(blank)`

    ❑ **Resource**: `/holiday-requests/v2`

    ❑ **Body**: This is given by the following code:

    ```
    <holidayRequest>
      <employeeId>300</employeeId>
      <employeeName>Jackson Fredo</employeeName>
      <startDate>2014-06-19T00:00:00Z</startDate>
     <endDate>2014-06-25T00:00:00Z</endDate>
    </holidayRequest>
    ```

12. Add **Regular Expression Extractor** to the **Create Holiday Request** HTTP sampler by navigating to **Create Holiday Request | Add | Post Processor | Regular Expression Extractor**.

13. Fill in the details for **Regular Expression Extractor** as follows:

    - **Reference Name**: `id`
    - **Regular Expression**: `<id>(\d+)</id>`
    - **Template**: `$1$`
    - **Match No.**: `0`
    - **Default Value**: `NOT_FOUND`

14. Add another **REST Sampler** component to **Thread Group** by navigating to **Thread Group | Add | Sampler | jp@gc – REST Sampler**. Fill in the details as follows:

    - **Name**: `Modify Holiday`
    - **Resource**: `/holiday-requests/v2`
    - **Method**: `PUT`
    - **Body Data**: This is given by the following code:

    ```
    <holidayRequest>
      <id>${id}</id>
      <employeeId>300</employeeId>
      <employeeName>Jackson Fredo</employeeName>
      <startDate>2014-07-19T00:00:00Z</startDate>
      <endDate>2014-07-25T00:00:00Z</endDate>
    </holidayRequest>
    ```

15. Add another **REST Sampler** component to **Thread Group** by navigating to **Thread Group | Add | Sampler | jp@gc – REST Sampler**. Fill in the details as follows:

    - **Name**: `Delete Holiday`
    - **Resource**: `/holiday-requests/v2/${id}`
    - **Method**: `DELETE`

16. Add a **View Results Tree** listener to the test plan by navigating to **Test Plan | Add | Listener | View Results Tree**.

17. Save and run the test plan. Observe the results of the execution.

How it works...

Since the service endpoints we tested in this recipe consumed and produced XML, we employed the REST Sampler and leveraged the main feature allowing us to easily interact with a service.

To test the various REST operations for create, read, update and delete (CRUD), we created a new test plan, added a **Thread Group** to it, and added a **REST Sampler** as a child component of the **Thread Group**. For reuse, we added a **User Defined Variable** component and **HTTP Head Manager** components to **Thread Group**. The former allows us to define common elements such as the host server, port, request parameters, and so on. The latter allows us to provide additional arguments or parameters to **HTTP Header**. This is not to be confused with request parameters. In our case, our service retrieves and sends XML, so we add a single entry, **Content-Type**: `application/xml`. With those set, we consume our service to retrieve some resources from a URI. To do this, we configured the path of the **REST Sampler** component we added to `/holiday-requests/v`. This takes care of getting all the vacations requested by employees. If we wanted to narrow this down and get a particular vacation, we could instead have used `/holiday-requests/v/id`, where `id` is the identifier of the target vacation.

In the same manner, we provided requests to create, update, and delete a resource in steps 8, 10, and 11 respectively. We accomplished this by adding **REST Sampler** to **Thread Group** with the right HTTP methods accordingly. To create a new resource, we used POST and sent the XML representing the resource we wanted to create with the HTTP request. To update a resource, we used PUT and sent the updated resource with the request in XML format. Finally, to delete the resource, we sent a HTTP request to `/holiday-requests/v/id` with a DELETE method, where `id` represented the resource to delete.

There's more...

It is not uncommon to encounter REST web services that are securely protected. Attempting to invoke such services without proper credentials will lead to an access denied error. As such, we have to properly send across the credentials with each request we make to such secured services. Often, this can be accomplished by adding **HTTP Header Properties** representing validation tokens along with each request. Just like we added a header property to denote that we will be receiving and sending XML messages to our service, we can add additional header properties to represent such tokens. These tokens vary from service to service, so be sure to consult the API vendor for the valid properties to set when testing them.

See also

▶   *Chapter 4, Testing Services*.

Using Ultimate Thread Group

At times, you might need more fine-grained control over your thread groups. You may need to define initial delays and the run duration for your threads. Also, you may need to specify separate scheduled records with different values for each of the previously mentioned properties. This is exactly what Ultimate Thread Group does. It allows you to define an infinite number of schedule records with different ramp-up times, shutdown times, and flight times while providing you with a load preview graph. This can help you define test plans that fit realistic use cases.

How to do it...

In this recipe, we will see how we can use Ultimate Thread Group in our test plans. Perform the following steps:

1. Download the standard set of plugins from `http://jmeter-plugins.org/`.
2. Install the plugins by doing the following:

    1. Extract the ZIP archive to the location of your choice.
    2. Copy the JAR file contained in `lib/ext` folder of the extract location to `$JMETER_HOME/lib/ext` directory.
    3. Copy all the JAR files from the `lib` directory of the extracted location to the `$JMETER_HOME/lib` directory.

3. Launch JMeter.
4. Add **jp@gc - Ultimate Thread Group** by navigating to **Test Plan | Add | Threads(Users) | jp@gc - Ultimate Thread Group**.
5. Click on the **Add Row** button three times to add three separate scheduled records.
6. Fill in the details as follows:

Start Threads Count	Initial Delay, sec	Start Time, sec	Hold Load For, sec	Shutdown Time
100	0	30	60	10
100	20	45	40	10
50	40	0	60	25

7. Add the **HTTP Request** component to the thread group by navigating to **jp@gc - Ultimate Thread Group | Add | Sampler | HTTP Request**.

8. Fill in the following details:

   ❑ **Server Name or IP**: api-jcb.herokuapp.com

   ❑ **Method**: GET

   ❑ **Path**: /holiday-requests

9. Add the **Aggregate Report** listener to the test plan by navigating to **jp@gc - Ultimate Thread Group | Add | Listener | Aggregate Report**.

10. Run the test and observe the result. This is shown in the following screenshot:

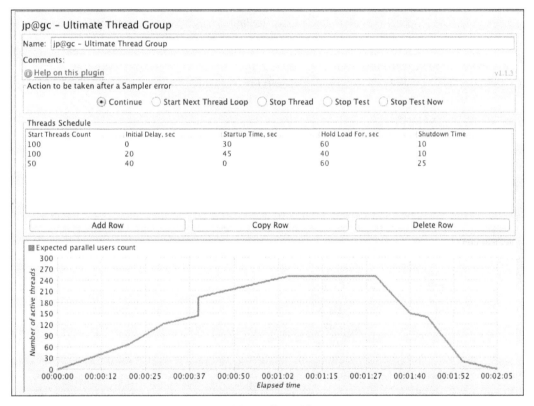

Using Ultimate Thread Group

How it works...

We extended JMeter by downloading and installing extensions from the JMeter plugin website. Once installed, we had additional components to add to our test plans. One such component is **Ultimate Thread Group**. We created a new test plan and added this component to it. We then defined three separate scheduled records within the **Ultimate Thread Group** component. In our case, this gave us a total of 250 simulated users. The first scheduled record starts 100 users within 30 seconds, executes the test for 60 seconds, and shuts them down within 10 seconds. The second scheduled record starts another set of 100 users (with a delay of 20 seconds) within 45 seconds, executes the test for 40 seconds, and shuts them down within 10 seconds. The third scheduled record starts the last set of 50 users (with a delay of 40 seconds) at once, executes the test for 60 seconds, and shuts them down within 25 seconds.

This gave us the load preview graph illustrated in the previous screenshot. With that set, we added a **HTTP Request Sampler** component and a result listener to our test plans. Once executed, we were able to observe what the test plan did and whether it was exactly as we expected.

See also

Among the additional components provided by the extension is **Stepping Thread Group**. This component provides a thread-scheduling algorithm similar to what users of HP's LoadRunner are used to. You can read more about the details at `http://jmeter-plugins.org/wiki/SteppingThreadGroup/`.

Using Throughput Shaping Timer

Sometimes, stakeholders give you a projected target for several components within the system under load. For example, you might be told that at peak hours, the reporting module of an application receives high volumes of traffic, while the product viewing module receives much less traffic. With the help of network engineers, you will be able to come up with the number of requests per second during peak and off-peak hours for various modules within the application under test. However, once you have such numbers, it becomes increasingly difficult to tweak thread groups and timer delay settings within JMeter to simulate a targeted requests per second (RPS) value for the modules. This is exactly what the Throughput Shaping Timer component is for. It allows you to easily control a targeted RPS more easily.

How to do it...

In this recipe, we will show you how to leverage the Throughput Shaping Timer component in test plans. Perform the following steps:

1. Download the standard set of plugins from `http://jmeter-plugins.org/`.

2. Install the plugins by doing the following:

   ❑ Extract the ZIP archive to the location of your choice

   ❑ Copy the JAR file contained in `lib/ext` folder of the extract location to `$JMETER_HOME/lib/ext` directory

   ❑ Copy all the JAR files from the `lib` directory of the extracted location to `$JMETER_HOME/lib` directory

3. Launch JMeter.

4. Add **Thread Group** by navigating to **Test Plan | Add | Threads(Users) | Thread Group**.

5. Specify the following values for its attributes:

   ❑ **Number of Threads (users)**: `300`

   ❑ **Ramp-Up Period (in seconds)**: `45`

   ❑ **Loop count**: `Forever`

6. Add the **HTTP Request** component to **Thread Group** by navigating to **Thread Group | Add | Sampler | HTTP Request**.

7. Fill in the following details:

   ❑ **Server Name or IP**: `api-jcb.herokuapp.com`

   ❑ **Method**: `GET`

   ❑ **Path**: `/holiday-requests`

8. Add **Throughput Shaping Timer** to **Thread Group** by navigating to **Thread Group | Add | Timer | jp@gc - Throughput Shaping Timer**.

9. Click on the **Add Row** button five times to add five separate entry records.

10. Fill in the details as follows:

Start RPS	End RPS	Duration, sec
1	1000	120
1000	1000	60
1000	500	30
500	750	60
750	0	120

11. Add the **Transactions per Second** listener by navigating to **Thread Group | Add | Listener | jp@gc - Transactions per Second**.

12. Add the **Aggregate Report** listener by navigating to **Thread Group | Add | Listener | Aggregate Report**.

13. Run the test and observe the result as shown in the following screenshot:

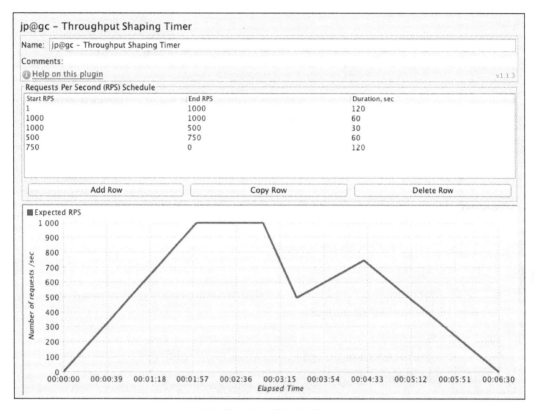

Using Throughput Shaping Timer

On running our test plan, our results look very close to what we set out to achieve, as observed in the following screenshot:

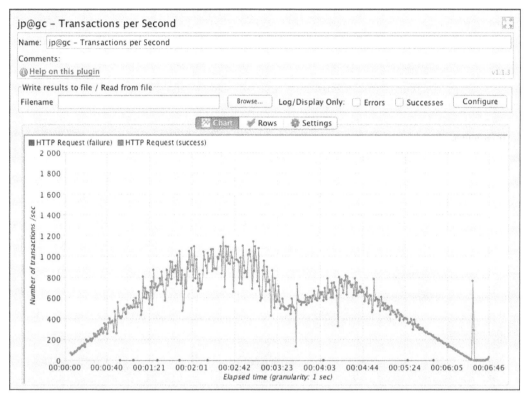

The Transactions per Second view of our test run

How it works...

Just as its name implies, the Throughput Shaping Timer add-on helps orchestrate threads, timer delay, and so on in a manner to ensure the desired throughput is attained (or as close to it as possible depending on server resources and other constraints). In our case, the goal was to test a REST endpoint and ensure it could handle as many as 1000 transactions per second under peak load. With the aid of the Throughput Shaping Timer component, we were able to configure our desired intent. We added several entries to the component. Each entry added specified a starting and ending **request per second** (**RPS**) and the duration it should be sustained for. The loading graph attached to the component helps visualize the load on the server over time.

After the execution of our test, we were able to verify our results by observing the Transaction per Second listener and see it closely mimic our intended load target.

The number of threads to attain the desired **transactions per second (TPS)** can be calculated as `RPS * max response time / 1000`.

See also

The full documentation of the Throughput Shaping Timer component can be found at `http://jmeter-plugins.org/wiki/ThroughputShapingTimer/`.

Using Console Status Logger

When executing JMeter tests (especially in non-GUI mode), it is helpful to get feedback on the terminal window regarding the progress and results of the tests. That is the main goal of the Console Status Logger component. This listener plugin prints short summary logs to the console while JMeter is running in non-GUI mode. In addition, the same info is written to the `jmeter.log` file when running in GUI mode.

How to do it...

In this recipe, we will use Console Status Logger to run a test in non-GUI mode. Perform the following steps:

1. Download the standard set of plugins from `http://jmeter-plugins.org/`.

2. Install the plugins by doing the following:

    ❑ Extract the ZIP archive to the location of your choice

    ❑ Copy the JAR file contained in `lib/ext` folder of the extract location to `$JMETER_HOME/lib/ext` directory

    ❑ Copy all the JAR files from the `lib` directory of the extracted location to the `$JMETER_HOME/lib` directory

3. Launch JMeter.

4. Open the `ch6_console_status_log.jmx` file bundled with the book's code samples.

5. Add the **jp@gc - Console Status Logger** component to the test plan by navigating to **Test Plan | Add | Listener | jp@gc - Console Status Logger**.

6. Close the JMeter GUI.

7. Run the test in non-GUI mode as shown in the following code snippet:

    ```
    ./jmeter -n -t [absolute path to script file]
    ./jmeter -n -t /workspace/packtpub/jmeter-cookbook/scripts/ch6/
    ch6_console_status_log.jmx
    ```

8. Observe the results in the terminal session. You should see an output similar to the following code snippet:

```
Starting the test @ Thu Jul 03 08:31:56 EDT 2014 (1404390716297)
Waiting for possible shutdown message on port 4445
#0      Threads: 10/50      Samples: 1    Latency: 13   Resp.Time:
693     Errors: 0
#1      Threads: 13/50      Samples: 30   Latency: 66   Resp.Time:
459     Errors: 0
#2      Threads: 18/50      Samples: 53   Latency: 34   Resp.Time:
262     Errors: 0
summary +      85 in   3.2s =    26.3/s Avg:    336 Min:    127 Max:
1743 Err:      0 (0.00%) Active: 18 Started: 18 Finished: 0
#3      Threads: 23/50      Samples: 69   Latency: 31   Resp.Time:
264     Errors: 0
#4      Threads: 28/50      Samples: 110  Latency: 19   Resp.Time:
221     Errors: 0
#5      Threads: 33/50      Samples: 106  Latency: 32   Resp.Time:
276     Errors: 0
#6      Threads: 37/50      Samples: 38   Latency: 116  Resp.Time:
656     Errors: 0
#7      Threads: 42/50      Samples: 152  Latency: 56   Resp.Time:
325     Errors: 0
#8      Threads: 47/50      Samples: 122  Latency: 36   Resp.Time:
352     Errors: 0
#9      Threads: 50/50      Samples: 215  Latency: 27   Resp.Time:
254     Errors: 0
...
summary +    3165 in    28s =  115.0/s Avg:    300 Min:    119 Max:
2079 Err:      0 (0.00%) Active: 0 Started: 50 Finished: 50
summary =    3250 in  30.1s =  108.0/s Avg:    301 Min:    119 Max:
2079 Err:      0 (0.00%)
Tidying up ...    @ Thu Jul 03 08:32:26 EDT 2014 (1404390746878)
... end of run
```

How it works...

Once added to a test plan, the Console Status Log listener prints short summary logs of the progress of the test to the console as it executes in non-GUI mode. The information printed includes the number of active threads running, the number of samples, the average response time, the error rate as a percentage, and the average latency time. This is slightly more expressive than the default output from JMeter. The following is a sample of the output from the same test execution without the Console Status Log listener:

```
Waiting for possible shutdown message on port 4445
summary +    1696 in  11.1s =  153.2/s Avg:    184 Min:    55 Max:   1208
Err:      0 (0.00%) Active: 47 Started: 50 Finished: 3
```

```
summary +    1554 in  20.1s =    77.4/s Avg:    303 Min:    55 Max:  1485
Err:       0 (0.00%) Active: 0 Started: 50 Finished: 50
summary =    3250 in  30.3s =   107.3/s Avg:    241 Min:    55 Max:  1485
Err:       0 (0.00%)
Tidying up ...      @ Thu Jul 03 08:40:19 EDT 2014 (1404391219234)
... end of run
```

 The same information printed to the console is also written to the `jmeter.log` file in GUI mode.

Using Dummy Sampler

Dummy Sampler is one of the most useful components you will come across. This sampler generates responses with the values already defined. For example, this can be very handy when used in combination with postprocessors such as the RegExp extractor, BeanShell postprocessor, CSS/JQuery extractor, BSF postprocessor, and so on. It cuts down script development and debugging time since you don't have to be repetitive with test executions or wait for certain conditions in the application under test to be met.

How to do it...

In this recipe, we will use Dummy Sampler with test plans to debug and extract information for a response using the BSF postprocessor. Perform the following steps:

1. Download the standard set of plugins from `http://jmeter-plugins.org/`.

2. Install the plugins by doing the following:

   ❑ Extract the ZIP archive to a location of your choice

   ❑ Copy the JAR file contained in `lib/ext` folder of the extracted location to the `$JMETER_HOME/lib/ext` directory

   ❑ Copy all the JAR files from the `lib` directory of the extracted location to the `$JMETER_HOME/lib` directory

3. Download the `groovy-all` JAR file from `http://devbucket-afriq.s3.amazonaws.com/jmeter-cookbook/groovy-all-2.3.3.jar`, or by searching "maven central" at `http://search.maven.org`, and add it to the `$JMETER_HOME/lib` directory.

4. Launch JMeter.

5. Add **Thread Group** by navigating to **Test Plan | Add | Threads(Users) | Thread Group**.

6. Add **Dummy Sampler** to **Thread Group** by navigating to **Thread Group | Add | Sampler | jp@gc - Dummy Sampler**.

7. In the **Response Data** text area, add the following content:

```
<records>
    <car name='HSV Maloo' make='Holden' year='2006'>
        <country>Australia</country>
        <record type='speed'>Production Pickup Truck with speed of
271kph</record>
    </car>
    <car name='P50' make='Peel' year='1962'>
        <country>Isle of Man</country>
        <record type='size'>Smallest Street-Legal Car at 99cm wide
and 59 kg in weight</record>
    </car>
    <car name='Royale' make='Bugatti' year='1931'>
        <country>France</country>
        <record type='price'>Most Valuable Car at $15 million</
record>
    </car>
</records>
```

8. Add **BSF PostProcessor** as a child of **Dummy Sampler** by navigating to
   jp@gc - Dummy Sampler | Add | Post Processors | BSF PostProcessor.

9. Select **groovy** as the language of choice in the **Language** drop-down box.

10. In the **Scripts** text area, add the following content:

```
def response = prev.getResponseDataAsString()
def slurper = new XmlSlurper()
def html = slurper.parseText(response)
def cars =
        html.car.collect {
            [
                    name: it.@name.text(),
                    make: it.@make.text(),
                    year: it.@year.text(),
                    country: it.country


            ]
        }

int count = 0
cars.each {
  vars.putObject("car_${count++}", it)
}
```

11. Add the **View Results Tree** listener to the test plan by navigating to **Test Plan | Add | Listener | jp@gc - Console Status Logger**.

12. Add the **Console Status Log** component to the test plan by navigating to **Test Plan | Add | Listener | View Results Tree**.

13. Add **Debug Sampler** to the test plan by navigating to **Test Plan | Add | Sampler | Debug Sampler**.

14. Run the test and observe the results.

How it works...

Our goal was to illustrate how the Dummy Sampler component could be used to generate a response and extract relevant information from the produced response. In step 6, we added a Dummy Sampler component to our test plan and filled the response with an XML response in step 7. Normally, such responses will be generated from the server in response to requesting a resource. With the response at hand, we then proceeded to add a postprocessor component to extract information from it. In our case, we chose **BSF PostProcessor**, but other postprocessors (depending on your needs) could have easily been used. For our sample response, we wanted to extract information such as the name, make, year, and country for as many cars as are in the response. Some of those details were nested within the response and might be cumbersome to extract without the powerful nature of **BSF PostProcessor**. In the end, we were able to extract the information we were interested in and publish them as JMeter variables, thereby making them available to other JMeter components that might wish to act on them further down the test plan.

There's more...

Though we entered an XML response in the Dummy Sampler component, it can handle any other type of responses including JSON, HTML, text, and so on. Also, Dummy Sampler allows you more fine-grained control over the response code, response message, response time, and latency of requests.

Developing custom JMeter plugins

One of the major benefits of using JMeter is that it is open source. As a result, it has a high level of community involvement that has lead to the creation of ample plugins that can be used to extend it and provide functionality that doesn't come out of the box. In the rare event that a plugin you need doesn't already exist, or the already existing one doesn't suit your needs, nothing stops you from creating one and contributing to the community. This is a huge win for JMeter over other closed commercial tools, as this opens up a new realm of possibilities.

How to do it...

JMeter comes bundled with an FTP sampler out of the box. In today's world of high secrecy, this protocol is too weak to use to transfer any kind of sensitive information between two machines, as information is not relayed over a secure channel and is thus subject to eavesdropping. To transfer files securely, we will develop a minimalistic SFTP component (credit goes to Yoann Ciabaud) that we can use within our test plans.

In this recipe, we will show you the process of developing a custom component. Perform the following steps:

1. Install JDK as described in the *Appendix*.

2. Install Gradle (a build tool) as described in the *Appendix*.

3. Create a new folder named `jmeter-sftp-sampler` on your machine. We will refer to this folder as `$ROOT_FOLDER`.

4. Open a terminal window and navigate to the location of `$ROOT_FOLDER`.

5. While in `$ROOT_FOLDER`, run the following command:

   ❑ On Unix:

   ```
   gradle init --type java-library
   ```

   ❑ On Windows:

   ```
   gradle.bat init --type java-library
   ```

6. Upon completion of this command, you will have a structure similar to the following code snippet:

   ```
   ├── build.gradle
   ├── gradle
   │   └── wrapper
   │       ├── gradle-wrapper.jar
   │       └── gradle-wrapper.properties
   ├── gradlew
   ├── gradlew.bat
   ├── settings.gradle
   └── src
       ├── main
       │   └── java
       │       └── Library.java
       └── test
           └── java
               └── LibraryTest.java
   7 directories, 8 files
   ```

7. Delete the `Library.java` and `LibraryTest.java` files as they are not needed. They are shown as follows:

   ❑ `rm src/main/java/Library.java`

   ❑ `rm src/test/java/LibraryTest.java`

8. Update the contents of the `build.gradle` file with the following:

```
apply plugin: 'java'
repositories {
    mavenCentral()
}
version = '0.1'
dependencies {
    compile 'org.slf4j:slf4j-api:1.7.5'
    testCompile 'junit:junit:4.11'
    compile('org.apache.jmeter:ApacheJMeter_core:2.11') {
        exclude module: 'rsyntaxtextarea'
    }
    compile 'com.fifesoft:rsyntaxtextarea:2.5.0'
    compile 'com.jcraft:jsch:0.1.51'
}
```

9. On the terminal, while at `$ROOT_FOLDER`, run `mkdir -p src/main/java/com/jcb/sampler` to create a package to hold the classes.

10. Create a file named `SFTPSampler.java` in the `com.jcb.sampler` package.

11. Copy the contents of `http://bit.ly/1mUCWKN` to the `SFTPSampler.java` file.

12. Create a file named `SFTPSamplerBeanInfo.java` in the `com.jcb.sampler` package.

13. Copy the contents of `http://bit.ly/1qIPrk6` to the `SFTPSamplerBeanInfo.java` file.

14. Create a file named `SFTPUserInfo.java` in the `com.jcb.sampler` package.

15. Copy the contents of `http://bit.ly/1omkmhi` to the `SFTPUserInfo.java` file.

16. Build a JAR by running `gradle build` from `$ROOT_FOLDER`.

17. Copy the newly created JAR (`$ROOT_FOLDER/build/libs/jmeter-sftp-sampler-0.1.jar`) to the `$JMETER_HOME/lib/ext` directory and `cp $ROOT_FOLDER/build/libs/jmeter-sftp-sampler-0.1.jar $JMETER_HOME/lib/ext`.

18. Launch JMeter.

19. Add **Thread Group** to the test plan by navigating to **Test Plan | Add | Threads(Users) | Thread Group**.

20. Verify our newly created component is available in the list of available samplers by navigating to **Thread Group** | **Add** | **Sampler** | **SFTPSampler**.

21. Use our sampler to upload or download files from an SFTP server by filling in the server details and relevant information.

How it works...

Since JMeter is pure Java, any extension in the form of plugins must compile down to byte code so that the **Java Virtual Machine** (**JVM**) can understand. So, it is no surprise that the first thing we needed to do was ensure we have a JDK installed on our system. The JDK allows us to write Java programs and also provides us ways to compile such programs to versions the JVM can execute. To take care of dependency management and building and packaging the application, we employed Gradle (`http://www.gradle.org/`), an incredibly powerful build tool for Java applications. Once Gradle was installed, we were able to use it to set up a standard Java project with a single command in step 4. In step 6, we deleted unneeded files put there by our initial setup command. Since we are building a plugin, in step 7, we added a dependency on JMeter core classes that is needed by all plugin extensions. Furthermore, since our aim was to build **Secure File Transfer Protocol** (**SFTP**) functionality, we added a dependency on the excellent JSCH library, a pure Java implementation of SSH2 (`http://www.jcraft.com/jsch/`). As a result of adding these dependencies, Gradle will take care of fetching all the JARs needed from external repositories and making them available in the classpath of our project.

With the required libraries out of the way, we proceeded to create a custom JMeter sampler in step 9. At minimum, to create a sampler, we need to have a class extend `AbstractSampler` and provide an implementation for the sample (entry) method. In this method, we provide implementation details of how the sampler should function and what we consider a failure or success of this sampler. At the end of the method's execution, we return an instance of `org.apache.jmeter.samplers.SampleResult`, which JMeter will use to report returns back to test plans. In our case, within the method, we make a secure SSH connection to a server and perform different operations based on the action configured by the user. This is where we leverage the JSCH library we added as a dependency earlier on.

In step 11, we created a class, `SFTPSamplerBeanInfo`, that extends `BeanInfoSupport`. This is not a mandatory class, but it was added to create logical groups of elements on the GUI, and also to set default values for certain elements within our sampler. The final class that we created, `SFTPUserInfo,` is just a supporting utility class for our sampler. It is an implementation of JSCH's `com.jcraft.jsch.UserInfo` and its sole purpose is to store password and passphrase entries from our sampler and use them when connecting to the server.

With all our classes in, we packaged our JAR by running `gradle build` and copied the resulting archive to the `JMETER_HOME/lib/ext` directory, making it available to JMeter. When we launched JMeter, we saw our sampler was now available to use and could now be used to securely transfer files between two servers.

There's more...

We have barely scratched the surface of what you can achieve by building your own JMeter plugins. What we built is a watered down version of the nice SSH sampler plugin by Yoann Ciabaud available at `https://github.com/yciabaud/jmeter-ssh-sampler`. We strongly encourage you to have a look at it and give it a try if you enjoy using it. There are ample samples on the Internet of various plugins, and we encourage you to look at their source code and gain insight from the wonderful work others have done. A good place to start will be looking at the samples provided with the JMeter official source code at `https://github.com/apache/jmeter/tree/docs-2.11/src/examples/org/apache/jmeter/examples/sampler`.

See also

A good way to get a grasp of developing custom plugins is to study the already existing ones out there. A good place to start is looking at the source code of the awesome JMeter-plugins extension at `https://github.com/undera/jmeter-plugins/`.

Also, check out the source code of JMeter at `https://github.com/apache/jmeter/`.

Additionally, check out the *Testing FTP services* recipe in *Chapter 4, Testing Services.*

Testing WebSocket-enabled applications

Another common wave of applications in today's flood of web applications is reactive real-time applications using WebSocket. WebSocket is a protocol that provides full-duplex bi-directional communication over a single TCP connection using default HTTP and HTTPS ports. Unlike other protocols, one connection is used for two-way communication for the WebSocket protocol. This makes it a good candidate for developing browser chat applications, gaming applications, real-time browser monitoring tools, and so on. It is supported on the majority of modern web browsers.

How to do it...

In this recipe, we will cover how to test WebSocket-enabled applications with JMeter:

1. Download the JMeter WebSocket Sampler component from `https://github.com/maciejzaleski/JMeter-WebSocketSampler/releases`.

2. Download the bundled ZIP containing the needed dependencies for the WebSocket Sampler component from `http://download.eclipse.org/jetty/updates/jetty-bundles-9.x/9.1.1.v20140108/`.

3. Install the WebSocket Sampler component by doing the following:

    1. Place the downloaded JAR from step 1 into the `$JMETER_HOME/lib/ext` directory.

    2. Place the dependencies specified in `https://github.com/maciejzaleski/JMeter-WebSocketSampler/wiki/Dependencies` (which are included as part of the ZIP file downloaded in step 2) into the `$JMETER_HOME/lib/ext` directory. The JARs should be similar to this listing:

        ```
        ├── org.eclipse.jetty.http_9.1.1.v20140108.jar
        ├── org.eclipse.jetty.io_9.1.1.v20140108.jar
        ├── org.eclipse.jetty.util_9.1.1.v20140108.jar
        ├── org.eclipse.jetty.websocket.api_9.1.1.v20140108.jar
        ├── org.eclipse.jetty.websocket.client_9.1.1.v20140108.jar
        └── org.eclipse.jetty.websocket.common_9.1.1.v20140108.jar
        ```

4. Launch (or restart) JMeter.

5. Add a new **Thread Group** to the newly created script by navigating to **Test Plan | Add | Threads (Users) | Thread Group**.

6. Add **WebSocket Sampler** to **Thread Group** by navigating to **Thread Group | Add | Sampler | WebSocket Sampler**.

7. Fill in the following details for the WebSocket Sampler component:

    ❑ **Server Name or IP**: `echo.websocket.org`

    ❑ **Streaming connection**: `checked`

    ❑ **Request data**: `Websocket request from JMeter`

8. Add the **View Results Tree** listener to the test script by navigating to **Test Plan | Add | Listener | View Results Tree**.

9. Save and run the test plan.

10. View the results in the listener and observe that the WebSocket request was successful, as shown in the following screenshot:

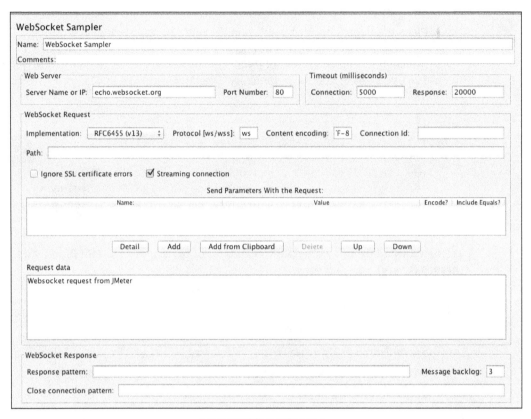

Using WebSocket Sampler

We extended JMeter with the WebSocket plugin (and its dependencies) to enable JMeter to understand how to correctly satisfy WebSocket requests. Once installed, we got a **WebSocket Sampler** that we then added to our test plan to make WebSocket requests. Each WebSocket request from a client starts with a HTTP request, provided the server understands the WebSocket protocol, and it upgrades the HTTP protocol into a WebSocket one during the handshaking phase of communication. All further communication between the client and the server is then transmitted over the WebSocket protocol using the token handed off to the client upon handshaking.

In our previous simple test case, the server echoes back any messages we sent it over the WebSocket protocol.

There's more...

`Socket.io` is a library written completely in JavaScript that uses the WebSocket protocol to communicate but falls back on other methods if needed. It comes in two flavors; a client-side library to run within the browser and a server-side library for Node.js. We can test applications that use Socket.io with JMeter. To do so, we have to fully simulate the chain of processes needed to communicate successfully at that level. This includes the initial HTTP request, the handshake process (switching from HTTP to the WebSocket protocol), the connection to the server with the token retrieved from the handshaking step, the event handling (for example, sending a message), and disconnecting from the server when done. Our test is that of a minimal chat application that uses `Socket.io` at its core. Take a look at the sample application at `http://chattybox.herokuapp.com` and the test script written for it in `scripts/ch6/websocket_02.jmx`.

See also

You can read more about WebSocket and `socket.io` at `http://www.websocket.org` and `https://github.com/automattic/socket.io-protocol`.

7
Building, Debugging, and Analyzing the Results of Test Plans

In this chapter, we will cover the following recipes:

- ▶ Using the View Results Tree listener
- ▶ Using the Aggregate Report listener
- ▶ Debugging with Debug Sampler
- ▶ Using Constant Throughput Timer
- ▶ Using the JSR223 postprocessor
- ▶ Analyzing Response Times Over Time
- ▶ Analyzing transactions per second
- ▶ Using User Defined Variables (UDV)

Introduction

One of the critical aspects of performance testing is knowing the right tools to use to attain your desired targets. Even when you settle on a tool, it is helpful to understand its features, component sets, and extensions, and appropriately apply them when needed.

In this chapter, we will go over some helpful components that will aid you in recording robust and realistic test plans while effectively analyzing reported results. We will also cover some components to help you debug test plans.

Using the View Results Tree listener

One of the most often used listeners in JMeter is the View Results Tree listener. This listener shows a tree of all sample responses, giving you quick navigation of any sample's response time, response codes, response content, and so on. The component offers several ways to view the response data, some of which allow you to debug CSS/jQuery, regular expressions, and XPath queries, among other things. In addition, the component offers the ability to save responses to file, in case you need to store them for offline viewing or run some other processes on them. Along with the various bundled testers, the component provides a search functionality that allows you to quickly search for the responses of relevant items.

How to do it...

In this recipe, we will cover how to add the View Results Tree listener to a test plan and then use its in-built testers to test the response and derive expressions that we can use in postprocessor components. Perform the following steps:

1. Launch JMeter.

2. Add **Thread Group** to the test plan by navigating to **Test Plan | Add | Threads (Users) | Thread Group**.

3. Add **HTTP Request** to the thread group by navigating to **Thread Group | Add | Sampler | HTTP Request**.

4. Fill in the following details:

   ❑ **Server Name or IP**: `dailyjs.com`

5. Add the **View Results Tree** listener to the test plan by navigating to **Test Plan | Add | Listener | View Results Tree**.

6. Save and run the test plan.

7. Once done, navigate to the **View Results Tree** component and click on the **Response Data** tab.

8. Observe some of the built-in renders.

9. Switch to the HTML render view by clicking on the dropdown and use the search textbox to search for any word on the page.

10. Switch to the HTML (download resources) render view by clicking on the dropdown.

11. Switch to the XML render view by clicking on the dropdown. Notice the entire HTML DOM structure is presented as the XML node elements.

12. Switch to the RegExp Tester render view by clicking on the dropdown and try out some regular expression queries.

13. Switch to the XPath Query Tester render view and try out some XPath queries.

14. Switch to the CSS/jQuery Tester render view and try out some jQuery queries, for example, selecting all links inside `divs` marked with a class preview (**Selector**: `div.preview a`, **Attribute**: `href`, **CSS/jQuery Implementation**: `JSOUP`).

How it works...

As your test plans execute, the **View Result Tree** listener reports each sampler in your test plans individually. The **Sampler Result** tab of the component gives you a summarized view of the request and response including information such as load time, latency, response headers, body content sizes, response code and messages, response header content, and so on. The **Request** tab shows the actual request that got fulfilled by the sampler, which could be any of the acceptable requests the server can fulfill (for example, GET, POST, PUT, DELETE, and so on) along with details of the request headers. Finally, the **Response Data** tab gives the rendered view of the response received back from the server. The component includes several built-in renders along with tester components (CSS/JQuery, RegExp, and XPath) that allow us to test and come up with the right expressions or queries needed to use in postprocessor components within our test plans. This is a huge time saver as it means we don't have to exercise the same tests repeatedly to nail down such expressions.

There's more...

As with most things bundled with JMeter, additional view renders can be added to the **View Result Tree** component. The defaults included are Document, HTML, HTML (download resources), JSON, Text, and XML. Should any of these not suit your needs, you can create additional ones by implementing `org.apache.jmeter.visualizers.ResultRender` interface and/or extending `org.apache.jmeter.visualizers.SamplerResultTab abstract class`, bundling up the compiled classes as a JAR file and placing them in the `$JMETER_HOME/lib/ext` directory to make them available for JMeter.

 The **View Result Tree** listener consumes a lot of memory and CPU resources, and should not be used during load testing. Use it only to debug and validate the test plans.

See also

▸ The *Debugging with Debug Sampler* recipe

▸ The detailed component reference for the **View Results Tree** listener can be found at `http://jmeter.apache.org/usermanual/component_reference.html#View_Results_Tree`.

Using the Aggregate Report listener

Another often used listener in JMeter is the Aggregate Report listener. This listener creates a row for each uniquely named request in the test plan. Each row gives a summarized view of useful information including **Request Count, Average, Median, Min, Max, 90% Line, Error Rate, Throughput, Requests/second**, and **KB/sec**. The **90% Line** column is particularly worth paying close attention to as you execute your tests. This figure gives you the time it takes for the majority of threads/users to execute a particular request. It is measured in milliseconds. Higher numbers here are indicative of slow requests and/or components within the application under test.

Equally important is the **Error** % column, which reports the failure rate of each sampled request. It is reasonable to have some level of failure when exercising test runs, but too high a number is an indication of either errors in scripts or certain components in the application under test. Finally, of interest to stack holders might be the number of requests per second, which the **Throughput** column reports. The throughput values are approximate and let you know just how many requests per second the server is able to handle.

How to do it...

In this recipe, we will cover how to add an **Aggregate Report** listener to a test plan and then see the summarized view of our execution:

1. Launch JMeter.
2. Open the `ch7_shoutbox.jmx` script bundled with the code samples. Alternatively, you can download it from `https://github.com/jmeter-cookbook/bundled-code/scripts/ch7/ch7_shoutbox.jmx`.
3. Add the **Aggregate Report** listener to **Thread Group** by navigating to **Thread Group | Add | Listener | Aggregate Report**.
4. Save and run the test plan.
5. Observe the real-time summary of results in the listener as the test proceeds.

How it works...

As your test plans execute, the **Aggregate Report** listener reports each sampler in your test plan on a separate row. Each row is packed with useful information. The **Label** column reflects the sample name, **# Samples** gives a count of each sampler, and **Average, Mean, Min,** and **Max** all give you the respective times of each sampler. As mentioned earlier, you should pay close attention to the **90% Line** and **Error** % columns. This can help quickly pinpoint problematic components within the application under test and/or scripts. The **Throughput** column gives an idea of the responsiveness of the application under test and/or server. This can also be indicative of the capacity of the underlying server that the application under test runs on. This entire process is demonstrated in the following screenshot:

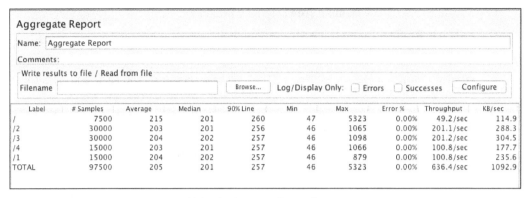

Label	# Samples	Average	Median	90% Line	Min	Max	Error %	Throughput	KB/sec
/	7500	215	201	260	47	5323	0.00%	49.2/sec	114.9
/2	30000	203	201	256	46	1065	0.00%	201.1/sec	288.3
/3	30000	204	202	257	46	1098	0.00%	201.2/sec	304.5
/4	15000	203	201	257	46	1066	0.00%	100.8/sec	177.7
/1	15000	204	202	257	46	879	0.00%	100.8/sec	235.6
TOTAL	97500	205	201	257	46	5323	0.00%	636.4/sec	1092.9

Using the Aggregate Report listener

See also

▶ http://jmeter.apache.org/usermanual/component_reference.html#Summary_Report.

Debugging with Debug Sampler

Often, in the process of recording a new test plan or modifying an existing one, you will need to debug the scripts to finally get your desired results. Without such capabilities, the process will be a mix of trial and error and will become a time-consuming exercise. Debug Sampler is a nifty little component that generates a sample containing the values of all JMeter variables and properties. The generated values can then be seen in the **Response Data** tab of the **View Results Tree** listener. As such, to use this component, you need to have a **View Results Tree** listener added to your test plan. This component is especially useful when dealing with postprocessor components as it helps to verify the correct or expected values that were extracted during the test run.

How to do it...

In this recipe, we will see how we can use Debug Sampler to debug a postprocessor in our test plans. Perform the following steps:

1. Launch JMeter.
2. Open the prerecorded script ch7_debug_sampler.jmx bundled with the book. Alternatively, you can download it from http://git.io/debug_sampler.
3. Add **Debug Sampler** to the test **Thread Group** by navigating to **Thread Group** | **Add** | **Sampler** | **Debug Sampler**.
4. Save and run the test.

5. Navigate to the **View Results Tree** listener component.

6. Switch to **RegExp Tester** by clicking on the dropdown.

7. Observe the response data of the **Get All Requests** sampler.

8. What we want is a regular expression that will help us extract the ID of entries within this response. After a few attempts, we settle at `"id": (\d+)`.

9. Enable all the currently disabled samplers, that is, **Request/Create Holiday Request**, **Modify Holiday**, **Get All Requests**, and **Delete Holiday Request**.

10. You can achieve this by selecting all the disabled components, right-clicking on them, and clicking on **Enable**.

11. Add the **Regular Expression Extractor** postprocessor to the **Request/Create Holiday Request** sampler by navigating to **Request/Create Holiday Request | Add | Post Processors | Regular Expression Extractor**.

12. Fill in the following details:

    - **Reference Name**: id
    - **Regular Expression**: `"id": (\d+)`
    - **Template**: 1
    - **Match No.:** 0
    - **Default Value**: NOT_FOUND

13. Save and rerun the test.

14. Observe the ID of the newly created holiday request and whether it was correctly extracted and reported in **Debug Sampler**.

How it works...

Our goal was to test a REST API endpoint that allows us to list, modify, and delete existing resources or create new ones. When we create a new resource, the identifier (ID) is autogenerated from the server. To perform any other operations on the newly created resource, we need to grab its autogenerated ID, store that in a JMeter variable, and use it further down the execution chain. In step 7, we were able to observe the format of the server response for the resource when we executed the **Get All Requests** sampler. With the aid of **RegExp Tester**, we were able to nail down the right regular expression to use to extract the ID of a resource, that is, `"id": (\d+)`. Armed with this information, we added a **Regular Expression Extractor** postprocessor component to the **Request/Create Holiday Request** sampler and used the derived expression to get the ID of the newly created resource. We then used the ID stored in JMeter to modify and delete the resource down the execution chain. After test completion, with the help of **Debug Sampler**, we were able to verify whether the resource ID was properly extracted by the **Regular Expression Extractor** component and stored in JMeter as an ID variable.

Using Constant Throughput Timer

While running test simulations, it is sometimes necessary to be able to specify the throughput in terms of the number of requests per minute. This is the function of **Constant Throughput Timer**. This component introduces pauses to the test plan in such a way as to keep the throughput as close as possible to the target value specified. Though the name implies it is constant, various factors affect the behavior, such as server capacity, other timers or time-consuming elements in the test plan, and so on. As a result, the targeted throughput could be lowered.

How to do it...

In this recipe, we will add **Constant Throughput Timer** to our test plan and see how we can specify the expected throughput with it. Perform the following steps:

1. Launch JMeter.

2. Open the prerecorded script `ch7_constant_throughput.jmx` bundled with the book. Alternatively, you can download it from `http://git.io/constant_throughput`.

3. Add **Constant Throughput Timer** to **Thread Group** by navigating to **Thread Group | Add | Timer | Constant Throughput Timer**.

4. Fill in the following details:
   - **Target throughput (in samples per minute)**: `200`
   - **Calculate Throughput based on**: `this thread only`

5. Save and run the test plan.

6. Allow the test to run for about 5 minutes.

7. Observe the result in the **Aggregate Result** listener as the test is going on.

8. Stop the test manually as it is currently set to run forever.

How it works...

The goal of the **Constant Throughput Timer** component is to get your test plan samples as close as possible to a specified desired throughput. It achieves this by introducing variable pauses to the test plan in such a manner that will keep numbers as close as possible to the desired throughput. That said, throughput will be lowered if the server resources of the system under test can't handle the load. Also, other elements (for example, other timers, the number of specified threads, and so on) within the test plan can affect attaining the desired throughput.

In our recipe, we have specified the throughput rate to be calculated based on a single thread, but **Constant Throughput Timer** also allows throughput to be calculated based on all active threads and all active threads in the current thread group. Each of these settings can be used to alter the behavior of the desired throughput.

 As a rule of thumb, avoid using other timers at the same time you use Constant Throughput Timer, since you'll not achieve the desired throughput.

See also

▸ The *Using Throughput Shaping Timer* recipe in *Chapter 6, Extending JMeter*

▸ `http://jmeter.apache.org/usermanual/component_reference.html#timers`

Using the JSR223 postprocessor

The JSR223 postprocessor allows you to use precompiled scripts within test plans. The fact that the scripts are compiled before they are actually used brings a significant performance boost compared to other postprocessors. This also allows a variety of programming languages to be used, including Java, Groovy, BeanShell, JEXL, and so on. This allows us to harness the powerful language features in those languages within our test plans.

JSR223 components, for example, could help us tackle preprocessor or postprocessor elements and samplers, allowing us more control over how elements are extracted from responses and stored as JMeter variables.

How to do it...

In this recipe, we will see how to use a JSR223 postprocessor within our test plan. We have chosen Groovy (`http://groovy.codehaus.org/`) as our choice of scripting language, but any of the other supporting languages will do:

1. Download the standard set of plugins from `http://jmeter-plugins.org/`.

2. Install the plugins by doing the following:

    ❑ Extract the ZIP archive to the location of your chosen directory

    ❑ Copy the `lib` folder in the extracted directory into the `$JMETER_HOME` directory

3. Download the `groovy-all` JAR file from `http://devbucket-afriq.s3.amazonaws.com/jmeter-cookbook/groovy-all-2.3.3.jar` and add it to the `$JMETER_HOME/lib` directory.

4. Launch JMeter.

5. Add **Thread Group** by navigating to **Test Plan | Add | Threads(Users) | Thread Group**.

6. Add **Dummy Sampler** to **Thread Group** by navigating to **Thread Group | Add | Sampler | jp@gc - Dummy Sampler**.

7. In the **Response Data** text area, add the following content:

```
<records>
    <car name='HSV Maloo' make='Holden' year='2006'>
        <country>Australia</country>
        <record type='speed'>Production Pickup Truck with speed of
271kph</record>
    </car>
    <car name='P50' make='Peel' year='1962'>
        <country>Isle of Man</country>
        <record type='size'>Smallest Street-Legal Car at 99cm wide
and 59 kg in weight</record>
    </car>
    <car name='Royale' make='Bugatti' year='1931'>
        <country>France</country>
        <record type='price'>Most Valuable Car at $15 million</
record>
    </car>
</records>
```

8. Download the Groovy script file from `http://git.io/8jCXMg` to any location of your choice. Alternatively, you can get it from the code sample bundle accompanying the book (`ch7_jsr223.groovy`).

9. Add **JSR223 PostProcessor** as a child of **Dummy Sampler** by navigating to **jp@gc - Dummy Sampler | Add | Post Processors | JSR223 PostProcessor**.

10. Select Groovy as the language of choice in the **Language** drop-down box.

11. In the **File Name** textbox, put in the absolute path to where the Groovy script file is, for example, `/tmp/scripts/ch7/ch7_jsr223.groovy`.

12. Add the **View Results Tree** listener to the test plan by navigating to **Test Plan | Add | Listener | View Results Tree**.

13. Add **Debug Sampler** to **Thread Group** by navigating to **Thread Group | Add | Sampler | Debug Sampler**.

14. Save and run the test.

15. Observe the **Response Data** tab of **Debug Sampler** and see how we now have the JMeter variables `car_0`, `car_1`, and `car_2`, all extracted from the **Response Data** tab and populated by our JSR223 postprocessor component.

How it works...

JMeter exposes certain variables to the JSR223 component, allowing it to get hold of sample details and information, perform logic operations, and store the results as JMeter variables. The exposed attributes include **Log**, **Label**, **Filename**, **Parameters**, **args[]**, **ctx**, **vars**, **props**, **prev**, **sampler**, and **OUT**. Each of these allows access to important and useful information that can be used during the postprocessing of sampler responses.

The log gives access to **Logger** (an instance of an Apache Commons Logging log instance; see `http://bit.ly/1xt5dmd`), which can be used to write log statements to the logfile. The **Label** and **Filename** attributes give us access to the sample label and script file name respectively. The **Parameters** and **args[]** attributes give us access to parameters sent to the script. The **ctx** attribute gives access to the current thread's JMeter context (`http://bit.ly/11M31MC`). **vars** gives access to write values into JMeter variables (`http://bit.ly/1o5DDBr`), exposing them to the result of the test plan. The **props** attribute gives us access to JMeterProperties. The **sampler** attribute gives us access to the current sampler while **OUT** allows us to write log statements to the standard output, that is, `System.out`. Finally, the **prev** sample gives access to previous sample results (`http://bit.ly/1rKn8Cs`), allowing us to get useful information such as the response data, headers, assertion results, and so on.

In our script, we made use of the **prev** and **vars** attributes. With **prev**, we were able to get hold of the XML response from the sample. Using Groovy's XmlSlurper (`http://bit.ly/1AoRMnb`), we were able to effortlessly process the XML response and compose the interesting bits, storing them as JMeter variables using the **vars** attribute.

Using this technique, we are able to accomplish tasks that might have otherwise been cumbersome to achieve using any other postprocessor elements we have seen in other recipes. We are able to take full advantage of the language features of any chosen scripting language. In our case, we used Groovy, but any other supported scripting languages you are comfortable with will do as well.

See also

- `http://jmeter.apache.org/api`
- `http://jmeter.apache.org/usermanual/component_reference.html#BSF_PostProcessor`
- `http://jmeter.apache.org/api/org/apache/jmeter/threads/JMeterContext.html`
- `http://jmeter.apache.org/api/org/apache/jmeter/threads/JMeterVariables.html`
- `http://jmeter.apache.org/api/org/apache/jmeter/samplers/SampleResult.html`

Analyzing Response Times Over Time

An important aspect of performance testing is the response times of the application under test. As such, it is often important to visually see the response times over a duration of time as the test plan is executed. Out of the box, JMeter comes with the Response Time Graph listener for this purpose, but it is limited and lacks some features. Such features include the ability to focus on a particular sample when viewing chat results, controlling the granularity of timeline values, selectively choosing which samples appear or not in the resulting chart, controlling whether to use relative graphs or not, and so on. To address all these and more, the Response Times Over Time listener extension from the JMeter plugins project comes to the rescue. It shines in areas where the Response Time Graph falls short.

How to do it...

In this recipe, we will see how to use the Response Times Over Time listener extension in our test plan and get the response times of our samples over time. Perform the following steps:

1. Download the standard set of plugins from `http://jmeter-plugins.org/`.

2. Install the plugins by doing the following:

    ❑ Extract the ZIP archive to the location of your chosen directory

    ❑ Copy the `lib` folder in the extracted directory into the `$JMETER_HOME` directory

3. Launch JMeter.

4. Open any of your existing prerecorded scripts or record a new one. Alternatively, you can open the `ch7_response_times_over_time.jmx` script accompanying the book or download it from `http://git.io/response_times_over_time`.

5. Add the **Response Times Over Time** listener to the test plan by navigating to **Test Plan | Add | Listener | jp@gc - Response Times Over Time**.

6. Save and execute the test plan.

7. View the resulting chart in the tab by clicking on the **Response Times Over Time** component.

8. Observe the time elapsed on the x axis and the response time in milliseconds on the y axis for all samples contained in the test plan.

9. Navigate to the **Rows** tab and exclude some of the samples from the chart by unchecking the selection boxes next to the samples.

10. Switch back to the **Chart** tab and observe that the chart now reflects your changes, allowing you to focus in on interested samples.

11. Switch to the **Settings** tab and see all the available configuration options.

12. Change some options and repeat the test execution. This is shown in the following screenshot:

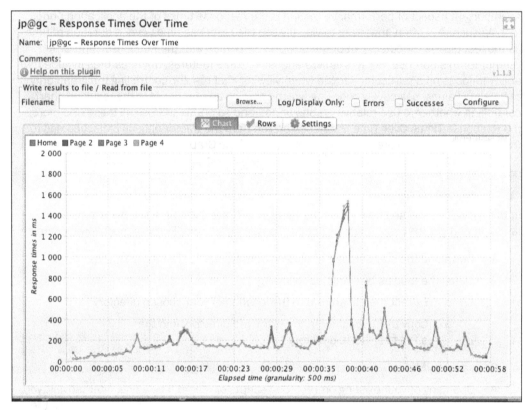

Analyzing Response Times Over Time

How it works...

Just like its name implies, the Response Times Over Time listener extension displays the average response time in milliseconds for each sampler in the test plan. It comes with various configuration options that allow you to customize the resulting graph to your heart's content. More importantly, it allows you to focus in on specific samples in your test plan, helping you pinpoint potential bottlenecks or problematic modules within the application under test.

For graphs to be more meaningful, it helps to give samples sensible descriptive names and tweak the granularity of the elapsed time to a higher number in the **Settings** tab if you have long running tests. After test execution, data of any chart can also be exported to a CSV file for further analysis or use as you desire.

Any listener that charts results will have some impact on performance and shouldn't be used during high volume load testing.

Analyzing transactions per second

Sometimes we are tasked with testing backend services, application program interfaces (APIs), or some other components that may not necessarily have a graphical user interface (GUI) attached to it, for example, a classic web application. At such times, the measure of the responsiveness of the module, for example, will be how many transactions per second it can withstand before slowness is observed. For example, **transactions per second** (**TPS**) is useful information for stakeholders who are providing services that can be consumed by various third-party components or other services. Good examples of these include the Google search engine, which can be consumed by third-parties, and the Twitter and Facebook APIs, which allow developers to integrate their application with Twitter and Facebook respectively.

The transactions per second listener extension component from the JMeter plugins project allows us to measure the transactions per second. It plots a chart of the transactions per second over an elapsed duration of time.

How to do it...

In this recipe, we will see how to use the transactions per second listener extension in our test plan and get the transactions per second for a test API service:

1. Download the standard set of plugins from `http://jmeter-plugins.org/`.
2. Install the plugins by doing the following:
   - ❑ Extract the ZIP archive to the location of your chosen directory
   - ❑ Copy the `lib` folder in the extracted directory into the `$JMETER_HOME` directory
3. Launch JMeter.
4. Open the `ch7_transaction_per_sec.jmx` script accompanying the book or download it from `http://git.io/trans_per_sec`.
5. Add the **Transactions Per Second** listener to the test plan by navigating to **Test Plan | Add | Listener | jp@gc - Transactions per Second**.
6. Save and execute the test plan.
7. View the resulting chart in the tab by clicking on the **Transactions Per Second** component.
8. Observe the time elapsed on the *x* axis and the transactions/sec on the *y* axis for all samples contained in the test plan.

9. Navigate to the **Rows** tab and exclude some of the samples from the chart by unchecking the selection boxes next to the samples.

10. Switch back to the **Chart** tab and observe that the chart now reflects your changes, allowing you to focus in on interesting samples.

11. Switch to the **Settings** tab and see all the available configuration options.

12. Change some options and repeat the test execution.

How it works...

The transactions per second listener extension displays the transactions per second for each sample in the test plan by counting the number of successfully completed transactions each second. It comes with various configuration options that allow you to customize the resulting graph. Such configurations allow you to focus in on specific samples of interest in your test plan, helping you to get at impending bottlenecks within the application under test.

It is helpful to give your samples sensible descriptive names to help make better sense of the resulting graphs and data points. This is shown in the following screenshot:

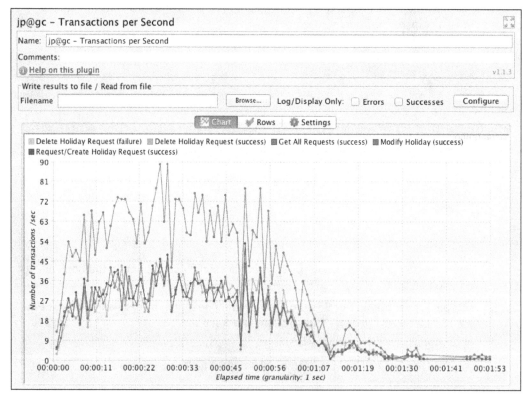

Analyzing transactions per second

Using User Defined Variables (UDV)

User Defined Variables (**UDVs**) are a great way to make test scripts more dynamic and robust. They allow you to define an initial set of variables, which can then be referenced in your test plans. When used with JMeter functions such as ___P(), they provide a means to update initially defined values from the command line without needing to modify the test script. Features such as this allow you to record a script against one environment (for example, a development environment) and then run it against a different environment (for example, Functional Test, UAT, and STAGE) at a later time. Also, UDVs allow you to extract common elements within your test plan into a centralized location, which makes your scripts a lot more maintainable.

All UDVs are evaluated at the start of the script regardless of where they are placed in the test plan. As a result, they cannot reference variables that are defined as part of the test run such as variables set during postprocessors. Additionally, it should be noted that UDVs shouldn't be used in combination with functions that change their results with each evaluation, as only the first evaluated value will be stored in the UDV.

 User Defined Variables are shared across thread groups, so be sure to use different names for different values when you have more than one thread group in your test plan.

How to do it...

In this recipe, you will learn how to use User Defined Variables to define some initial values that we will use within our test plan. Perform the following steps:

1. Launch JMeter.

2. Open the `ch7_user_defined_variables.jmx` script accompanying the book or download it from `http://git.io/user_defined_variables`.

3. Add the **User Defined Variables** component to the test plan by navigating to **Test Plan | Add | Config Element | User Defined Variables**.

4. Fill in the following details:

Name	Value
base_url	${__P(base_url, petclinic-jcb.herokuapp.com)}
num_of_users	${__P(num_of_users, 30)}
ramp_up	${__P(ramp_up, 20)}

5. Click on **Thread Group** and enter the following details:

   - **Number of Threads (users)**: `${num_of_users}`

   - **Ramp-Up Period (in seconds)**: `${ramp_up}`

6. Save and run the test.

7. Observe the results in the **Aggregate Report** listener.

How it works...

Once the prerecorded script was opened, we added a UDV component to our test plan. We then added some initial values of the target host and the number of users. The values we provided will be substituted anytime JMeter encounters the replacement token, that is, `${}`. As an example, if `anytime ${base_url}` is encountered in the test script, it will be replaced with `petclinic-jcb.herokuapp.com`, `${num_of_users}` with 30 and `${ramp_up}` with 20.

In addition, we are using the UDVs component with the `__P()` function. This gives us maximum flexibility, allowing us to override any value specified in the UDV component right from the command line at the time of script execution. As described earlier, this is useful for developing scripts once and then executing them against several environments. As an example, we could override the `base_url` by starting JMeter on the command line in the following way:

```
./jmeter -Jbase_url=prod.petclinic-jcb.io
```

UDVs are handy components that make our scripts more robust and maintainable.

 If a runtime element such as a postprocessor assigns a value to a variable with the same name as the one defined in the UDV, then this will also override the initial value set on the component.

8
Beyond the Basics

In this chapter, we will cover the following recipes:

- ▶ Continuous Integration with JMeter
- ▶ Testing with different bandwidths
- ▶ Using the HTTP Cache Manager component
- ▶ Using script languages within test plans
- ▶ Writing Test scripts through Ruby DSL
- ▶ Understanding JMeter properties
- ▶ Monitoring servers while executing tests (using VisualVM)
- ▶ Monitoring servers while executing tests (using YourKit Profiler)
- ▶ Monitoring servers while executing tests (using New Relic)
- ▶ Performance tips to scale JMeter

Introduction

There are quite a lot of tips and tricks for being more productive with JMeter. These include integrating it into your company's continuous integration pipeline, simulating varying connection bandwidths for threads, understanding and tweaking JMeter properties, getting the most out of JMeter when scaling it across multiple machine Instances, and much more.

In this chapter, we will go over some advance tips and see how we can enhance and have a much better experience with JMeter.

Continuous Integration with JMeter

Continuous Integration, or CI as it is often referred to, is a development practice that requires developers to integrate code into a shared repository several times a day. Each check-in is then verified by an automated build, allowing teams to detect problems early. This practice has been around since the late 90s, and more and more companies have embraced it so much that it has now become 'the de facto practice'.

As such, it would be advantageous and beneficial to have JMeter fit into this pipeline somehow. Wouldn't it be great to have performance tests automatically run on every code check-in to **version control system** (**VCS**) to know when an introduced change increased or decreased the application's performance? Such insights become indispensible as the application grows in complexity and help alleviate changes that will adversely impact the system from being introduced.

How to do it...

In this recipe, we will cover how to integrate JMeter into a continuous integration workflow and automatically test our application with each committed code change into the source repository. Perform the following steps:

1. Download Tomcat from `http://archive.apache.org/dist/tomcat/tomcat-8/v8.0.9/bin/apache-tomcat-8.0.9.zip` and extract it to a location of your choice. We will refer to this location as `$TOMCAT_HOME`. At the time of writing this, Tomcat 8 was the latest stable version, and that is what we will use.

2. Download the latest Jenkins WAR application from `http://mirrors.jenkins-ci.org/war/latest/jenkins.war` or download the native package for your operating system from `http://jenkins-ci.org/`. We will be following the WAR instruction throughout this recipe.

3. Copy the downloaded WAR in step 2 to the `$TOMCAT_HOME/webapps` directory.

4. Start Tomcat using the following command:

   cd $TOMCAT_HOME/bin

   - ❑ On Windows: `catalina.bat run`
   - ❑ On Unix: `./catalina.sh run`

5. If all goes well, you should see the following logs on your console:

   ```
   03-Aug-2014 07:56:28.263 INFO [main] org.apache.coyote.
   AbstractProtocol.init Initializing ProtocolHandler ["http-
   nio-8080"]
   ```
   ...

```
03-Aug-2014 07:56:28.391 INFO [localhost-startStop-1] org.apache.
catalina.startup.HostConfig.deployWAR Deploying web application
archive /Users/berinle/devtools/apache-tomcat-8.0.9/webapps/
jenkins.war
```

```
Jenkins home directory: /Users/berinle/.jenkins found at: $user.
home/.jenkins
```

```
03-Aug-2014 07:56:41.793 INFO [localhost-startStop-1] org.
apache.catalina.startup.HostConfig.deployWAR Deployment of web
application archive /Users/berinle/devtools/apache-tomcat-8.0.9/
webapps/jenkins.war has finished in 13,402 ms
```

```
03-Aug-2014 07:56:42.456 INFO [main] org.apache.catalina.startup.
Catalina.start Server startup in 14142 ms
```

...

```
03-Aug-2014 07:56:43.181 INFO [pool-5-thread-2] jenkins.
InitReactorRunner$1.onAttained Started initialization
```

```
03-Aug-2014 07:56:57.161 INFO [pool-5-thread-4] jenkins.
InitReactorRunner$1.onAttained Listed all plugins
```

```
03-Aug-2014 07:56:57.319 INFO [pool-5-thread-3] null.null Prepared
all plugins
```

```
03-Aug-2014 07:56:57.397 INFO [pool-5-thread-3] jenkins.
InitReactorRunner$1.onAttained Started all plugins
```

```
03-Aug-2014 07:56:57.480 INFO [pool-5-thread-3] null.null
Augmented all extensions
```

```
03-Aug-2014 07:56:57.492 INFO [pool-5-thread-2] null.null Loaded
all jobs
```

```
03-Aug-2014 07:57:08.085 INFO [SSHD.init] org.jenkinsci.main.
modules.sshd.SSHD.start Started SSHD at port 64181
```

```
03-Aug-2014 07:57:08.319 INFO [pool-5-thread-2] jenkins.
InitReactorRunner$1.onAttained Completed initialization
```

```
03-Aug-2014 07:57:08.448 INFO [Jenkins initialization thread]
hudson.WebAppMain$3.run Jenkins is fully up and running
```

6. Navigate to `http://localhost:8080/jenkins/` and verify that Jenkins is up.

7. Specify the location of your Maven install, that is, `$M2_HOME` or `$MAVEN_HOME`. Perform the following steps:

    ❑   Go to `http://localhost:8080/jenkins/configure`.

    ❑   Under the **Maven** section, enter a name and path of your maven home. Alternatively, you can also choose to automatically download and install maven as part of the installation if you don't already have it on your system.

    ❑   Click on the **Save** button.

8. Install the **Performance** test plugin add-on for Jenkins and perform the following steps:

    1. Click on the **Manage Jenkins** link in the left-hand sidebar.

    2. Click on the **Manage Plugins** link.

    3. Click on the **Available** tab and search for the **Performance** plugin by typing `performance` into the search box.

    4. Click on the **Install** checkbox next to the search box.

    5. Click on **Download now** and install after pressing the **Restart** button.

    6. Make sure you see the **Success** message, confirming the successful installation of the plugin.

    7. Restart the Tomcat server.

9. Go back to the Jenkins landing page at `http://localhost:8080/jenkins`.

10. Set up a new job by clicking on the **New Item** link.

11. Give any descriptive name for the new job, for example, `Cookbook API`.

12. Select the **Build a maven project radio** button.

13. Add two build parameters to **build** and perform the following steps:

    1. Check the **This build is parameterized** checkbox.

    2. Click on the **Add Parameter** button and select **Text Parameter**.

    3. Fill in `THREAD_COUNT` and `10` for the **Name** and **Default Value** textboxes respectively.

    4. Click on the **Add** Parameter button and select **Text Parameter**.

    5. Fill in `LOOP_COUNT` and `10` for the **Name** and **Default Value** textboxes respectively.

14. In the **Source Code Management** section, select **Git** and fill in the following details:

    ❑ **Repository URL**: `git@github.com:jmeter-cookbook/api-jcb.git`

    ❑ **Branch Specifier (blank for default)**: `origin/maven-build`

15. In the **Build** section, fill in the following under the **Goals** and **Options** textbox:

    ```
    clean -Pjenkins verify -Dperformancetest.threadCount=$THREAD_COUNT
    -Dperformancetest.loopCount=$LOOP_COUNT
    ```

16. Add **Post-Build Action** to view the performance test results, and then perform the following steps:

    1. Click on the **Add post-build action** button under the **Post-Build Actions** section.

    2. Click on the **Publish Performance** test result report option.

3. Click on the **Add a new report** drop-down and select **JMeter**. In the **Report files** textbox, enter `**/*.jtl`.

4. Click on the **Add a new report** drop-down and select **JmeterSummarizer**.

5. Fill in the following details:

   ❑ **Reports file**: `**/*.log`

   ❑ **Summarizer Date Format**: `yyyy/mm/dd HH:mm:ss`

   ❑ Under the **Use Error thresholds on single build** section, fill in the following details:

   Unstable: 2

   Failed: 5

   ❑ Under the **Use Relative thresholds for build comparison** section, fill in the following details:

   Unstable % Range: 1 and 5 respectively

   Failed % Range: 5 and 10 respectively

   ❑ Select the **Compare with previous Build radio** button

   ❑ Click on the **Save** button to save the configuration

17. Kick off a build by clicking on the **Run** button.

18. Specify the following build parameters:

    ❑ **THREAD_COUNT**: 50

    ❑ **LOOP_COUNT**: 10

19. Click on the **Build** button.

20. You can observe each step of the build process, including the performance tests run, by clicking on the **Console Output** link on the left side bar.

21. Once the build is complete, you can navigate the build workspace folder to see detailed HTML reports of the test run:

    ❑ Click on the `Workspace` folder link

    ❑ Click on the `target` folder link

    ❑ Click on the `api-jcb.html` link

    This gives a nice summary of the JMeter tests exercised along with a response times, status codes, and a graph. You can also drill down further to a detailed response information view from here by clicking on the buttons at the bottom of the page.

22. Observe the other graphs generated by the build process and perform the following steps:

    1. Click on the `Workspace` folder link.

    2. Click on the `target` folder link.

    3. Click on the `jmeter` folder link.

    4. Click on the `results` folder link.

    5. Click on the `api-jcb-ResponseTimesOverTime.png`, `api-jcb-TransactionsPerSecond.png`, and `api-jcb-ThreadsStateOverTime.png` links.

The following is a screenshot of the sample view of the requests duration graph generated for our test run:

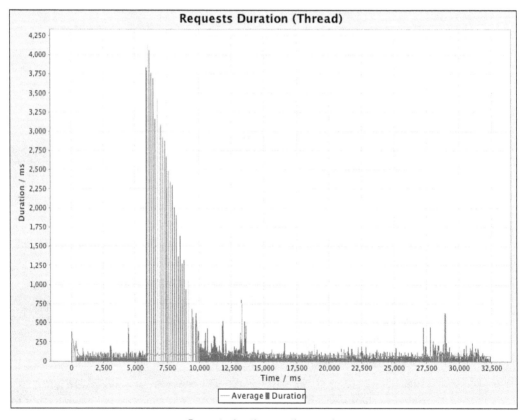

Requests duration over time graph

The following is a screenshot of the sample view of the transactions per second graph generated for our test run:

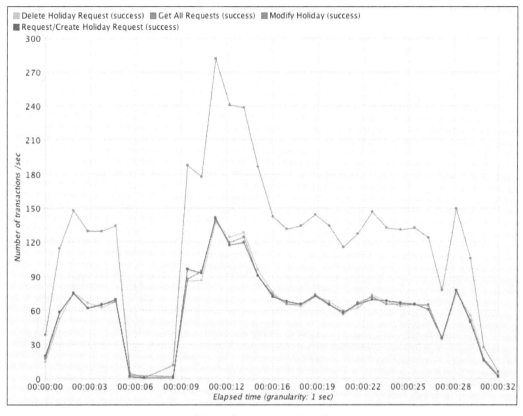

Transactions per second graph

How it works...

To integrate with a CI server, we first had to set up a local server. There are ample servers we could use for this, but the two most popular ones are Tomcat and Jetty. For illustrative purposes, we chose Tomcat. Once downloaded, we then deployed Jenkins to our Tomcat server by placing the already packaged WAR into the `webapps` directory of our Tomcat instance. Jenkins comes with quite a few plugins that add additional features. One of these plugins is the **Performance** plugin, which adds support for capturing reports from JMeter tests as part of our build process. We added this in step 8, since that is exactly what we intend to do. Running the actual test was configured as part of our build process with a maven plugin.

We then proceeded to add a new build job to Jenkins to instruct it in how exactly we want our project to be built. Along the way, we configured a parameterized build which allows us to dynamically configure how many threads and iterations run for each build.

With everything configured, we were able to kick off our build and observe the results of our test execution. Additionally, we verified the response times and other graphs we specified to be generated as part of our build process.

There's more...

We have cheated a bit here, since the test plan we are running in our Jenkins job is actually configured to run against an already deployed instance on Heroku, a Cloud platform. Ideally, we need our CI process to also deploy a new version of our project, which contains the new code changes to the server before proceeding to run our tests against it. This way, we can truly verify that the introduced change is in fact responsible for performance degradation or an increase. Doing this was a bit out of the scope of this book, so we decided not to include it. We will leave it as an exercise for the reader.

Additionally, we configured relative and error thresholds in step 14. Free feel to tweak this to suit the needs of your project. For example, your project could be more strict about what is considers as acceptable success. Maybe you want to mark a build as failed if there is any failure while exercising the JMeter tests as opposed to the 2-5 percent range we specified previously. For such instances, a build will be marked as failed if it even has as little as 0.1 percent of errors. For example, you might see this on the Jenkins console output if a build is marked as failed:

```
...

 [JENKINS] Archiving /Users/berinle/.jenkins/workspace/Cookbook
API (jmeter)/target/api-jcb-0.0.1.jar to com.jcb/api-jcb/0.0.1/
api-jcb-0.0.1.jar

channel stopped

Performance: Percentage of errors greater or equal than 0% sets
the build as unstable

Performance: Percentage of errors greater or equal than 0% sets
the build as failure

Performance: Recording JMeter reports '**/*.jtl'

Performance: Parsing JMeter report file /Users/berinle/.jenkins/
jobs/Cookbook API (jmeter)/builds/2014-08-20_05-46-35/performance-
reports/JMeter/api-jcb.jtl

api-jcb.jtl has an average of: 1259

Performance: File api-jcb.jtl reported 0.15% of errors [FAILURE].
Build status is: FAILURE
```

```
Performance: Recording JmeterSummarizer reports '**/*.log'

Performance: Parsing JMeterSummarizer report file api-jcb.jmx.log

Build step 'Publish Performance test result report' changed build
result to FAILURE

Finished: FAILURE
```

Finally, we could take things one step further and take advantage of Cloud CI services such as Travis CI (`https://travis-ci.org/`) or Drone.IO (`https://drone.io/`). Flood.IO, in fact, has a nice little integration with Travis CI in the form of webhooks. You can read more about that is `https://flood.io/blog/37-travis-ci-integration`. Blazemeter offers free Jenkins plugins, which enable your CI server to exercise your tests directly in the Cloud with each change to the repository.

See also

▸ The *Testing external facing applications with Flood.IO* recipe in *Chapter 5, Diving Into Distributed Testing*

▸ The *Writing Test scripts through Ruby DSL* recipe

▸ Flood.IO's Travis CI integration (`https://flood.io/blog/37-travis-ci-integration`)

▸ Loading testing in CI environments (`http://bit.ly/1vldvf1`)

▸ The BlazeMeter plugin for Jenkins (`http://bit.ly/1tBWx9Q`)

Testing with different bandwidths

To be certain that an application is ready to be shipped, one of the important aspects worth considering is how it will perform on different network speeds. For example, an application that shines when connecting from a really fast network such as an Ethernet or Fast Ethernet LAN might really underperform on a slow network such as a mobile EDGE or HSPA+ network for example. This could be a result of many things, including the amount of data being transferred across the network. The more data, the more latency and slowness will be seen on a slower network.

JMeter provides a way to simulate various network bandwidths, helping you to know exactly how the application under test will react under various network conditions. This is valuable information to stakeholders and helps teams plan ahead and put in place workarounds to give end users a better experience regardless of which device or network they are connecting from.

How to do it...

In this recipe, we will see how JMeter can be used to test at various bandwidths. Perform the following steps:

1. Open `$JMETER_HOME/bin/user.properties`.

2. Add the following properties to the end of the file (if they don't already exist). This specifies a mobile data GPRS: 171 Kbps bandwidth. Refer to the following parameters:

    - ❑ `httpclient.socket.http.cps=21888`
    - ❑ `httpclient.socket.https.cps=21888`

3. Save the file.

4. Launch JMeter.

5. Open the prerecorded script `ch8_bandwidth.jmx` bundled with the book. Alternatively, you can download it from **http://git.io/bandwidth**.

6. Run the test and observe the results in the Aggregate Report listener.

7. Pay special attention to the **KB/sec** column and notice JMeter tries as much as possible to throttle the bandwidth, keeping it as close as possible to the defined max of 171 kb/s.

8. Open `$JMETER_HOME/bin/user.properties`.

9. Modify the values of the CPS like so to specify a Wi-Fi 802.11a/g: 54 Mbps bandwidth:

    - ❑ `httpclient.socket.http.cps=6912000`
    - ❑ `httpclient.socket.https.cps=6912000`

10. Close and re-launch JMeter.

11. Repeat the last test.

12. Observe the values reported in the **KB/sec** column of the listener this time.

The following screenshot shows what our listener reported when we ran our test with a bandwidth of 171 Kbps:

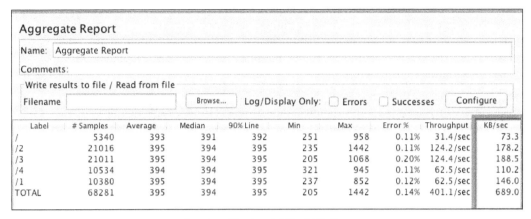

Label	# Samples	Average	Median	90% Line	Min	Max	Error %	Throughput	KB/sec
/	5340	393	391	392	251	958	0.11%	31.4/sec	73.3
/2	21016	395	394	395	235	1442	0.11%	124.2/sec	178.2
/3	21011	395	394	395	205	1068	0.20%	124.4/sec	188.5
/4	10534	394	394	395	321	945	0.11%	62.5/sec	110.2
/1	10380	395	394	395	237	852	0.12%	62.5/sec	146.0
TOTAL	68281	395	394	395	205	1442	0.14%	401.1/sec	689.0

Running with a bandwidth of 171 Kbps

The following screenshot shows what our listener reported when we ran our test with a bandwidth of 54 Mbps:

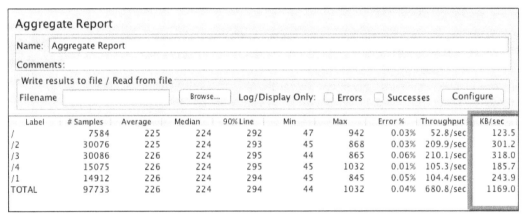

Label	# Samples	Average	Median	90% Line	Min	Max	Error %	Throughput	KB/sec
/	7584	225	224	292	47	942	0.03%	52.8/sec	123.5
/2	30076	225	224	293	45	868	0.03%	209.9/sec	301.2
/3	30086	226	224	295	44	865	0.06%	210.1/sec	318.0
/4	15075	226	224	295	45	1032	0.01%	105.3/sec	185.7
/1	14912	226	224	294	45	845	0.05%	104.4/sec	243.9
TOTAL	97733	226	224	294	44	1032	0.04%	680.8/sec	1169.0

Running with a bandwidth of 54 Mbps

Be sure to comment out or remove the newly added entries to `user.properties` once you are done with this recipe to avoid throttling other tests.

How it works...

With the addition/modification of two configuration settings in the `$JMETER_HOME/bin/user.properties` file, JMeter is able to throttle network bandwidth for our tests and give us some idea on how the application under test might or might not hold up under such bandwidths. It does this by delegating that responsibility to the underlining `Apache HttpComponents` implementation.

With our sample run as shown previously, we are able to observe just that. We can see a low percentage of errors reported for our mobile clients (that is, a bandwidth of 171 Kbps), while none is reported for our WIFI (that is, a bandwidth of 54 Mbps).

> The value for CPS we entered in the recipe is calculated as follows:
>
> `cps = (target bandwidth in kbps * 1024) / 8`

See also:

▶ Apache HTTP Components (`http://hc.apache.org/`)
▶ Controlling bandwidth in JMeter (`http://bit.ly/1otmUIz`)

Using the HTTP Cache Manager component

In practice, web browsers have a caching mechanism to reduce the amount of data transferred over the network. This in turn gives end users a better experience. If data has not changed since the first time it was fetched from the remote server, there is no point fetching it again and thus, it can be fetched from a locally cached copy of the browser.

This same behavior can also be achieved with JMeter using the HTTP Cache Manager component. With the HTTP Cache Manager configured, JMeter is able to cache responses from sampled requests and serve them back on subsequent requests if they have not changed on the remote server.

How to do it...

In this recipe, we will add an HTTP Cache Manager component to a test plan and observe the response times in comparison to it being disabled. Perform the following steps:

1. Launch JMeter.
2. Open the pre-recorded script `ch8_cache_manager.jmx` bundled with the book. Alternatively, you can download it from `http://git.io/cache_manager`.
3. Run the test plan and observe the result in the **View Results in Table** listener.

4. Add **HTTP Cache Manager** to **Test Plan** by navigating to **Test Plan | Add | Config Element | HTTP Cache Manager**.

5. Run the test and observe the results.

6. Click on the **HTTP Cache Manager** component and check the **Use Cache Control/Expires** header when processing the GET requests checkbox.

7. Run the test and observe the results.

How it works...

The HTTP Cache component primarily works with two attributes, **Last-Modified** and **Etag**. The **Last-Modified** header attribute denotes the date and time at which the origin server reports the resource that was last modified. The **Etag** response header provides the current value of the entity tag representing the resource and is used in conjunction with the **If-None-Match** header attribute.

The first time a resource is requested, JMeter saves the results in memory, that is, it writes it to RAM. **Last-Modified** and **Etag** are saved for the request. On subsequent requests, the sampler checks whether there is an entry in the cache, and if there is a hit, sets the **If-Last-Modified** and **If-None-Match** headers for the request.

As can be observed with our sample run, once the HTTP Cache Manager was added and we opted to use the cache control as done in step 6, the initial request took the most time. See the **Sample Time(ms)**, **Bytes**, and **Latency** columns of the **View Results in Table** listener. The remaining four calls made to the same URL are served from the cache and returned immediately. The **Sample Time (ms)**, **Bytes**, and **Latency** options are all 0 for those calls showing that no network latency was involved or data transferred. This mimics the exact behavior of a web browser, achieving exactly what we set out to do. This is shown in the following screenshot:

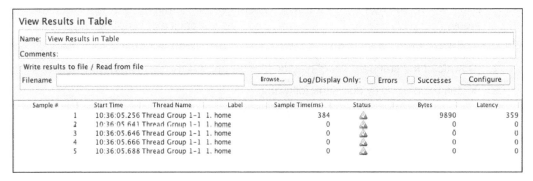

Using the HTTP Cache Manager

As a rule of thumb, different timers can be used within the same test plan.

See also

▸ HTTP ETag wiki (`http://en.wikipedia.org/wiki/HTTP_ETag`)

▸ HTTP Header Fields
  (`http://en.wikipedia.org/wiki/List_of_HTTP_header_fields`)

▸ Blog post: Using HTTP Cache Manager (`http://bit.ly/VOsET4`)

▸ Blog post: Understanding JMeter Cache (`http://bit.ly/1sA3839`)

Using script languages within test plans

JSR223 PostProcessor allows you to use precompiled scripts within test plans. The fact that the scripts are compiled before they are actually used brings a significant performance boost compared to their inline counter parts. This also allows a variety of scripting languages to be used including Java, groovy, beanshell, jexl, and so on, allowing us to harness the powerful language features in those languages within our test plan.

JSR223 components could, for example, help us tackle preprocessor or postprocessor elements, samplers, or completed or logical loops within our test plans, allowing us to have more control over how elements are extracted from responses and stored as JMeter variables.

How to do it...

In this recipe, we will see how to use a JSR223 postprocessor within our test plan. We have chosen groovy (`http://groovy.codehaus.org/`) as our choice of scripting language, but any of the other supporting languages will do. Perform the following steps:

1. Download the standard set of plugins from `http://jmeter-plugins.org/`.

2. Install the plugins by doing the following:

   ❑ Extract the ZIP archive to a location of your chosen directory

   ❑ Copy the JAR file contained in the `lib/ext` folder of the extract location to `$JMETER_HOME/lib/ext` directory

3. Download the groovy-all JAR (java archive) from `http://devbucket-afriq.s3.amazonaws.com/jmeter-cookbook/groovy-all-2.3.3.jar` or by searching maven central at the `http://search.maven.org` and add it to the `$JMETER_HOME/lib` directory.

4. Launch JMeter.

5. Add **Thread Group** to **Test Plan | Add | Threads(Users) | Thread Group**.

6. Add **Dummy Sampler** to **Thread Group** by navigating to **Thread Group | Add | Sampler | jp@gc - Dummy Sampler**.

7. In the **Response Data** text area, fill in the following contents:

```
<records>
    <car name='HSV Maloo' make='Holden' year='2006'>
        <country>Australia</country>
        <record type='speed'>Production Pickup Truck with speed of
271kph</record>
    </car>
    <car name='P50' make='Peel' year='1962'>
        <country>Isle of Man</country>
        <record type='size'>Smallest Street-Legal Car at 99cm wide
and 59 kg in weight</record>
    </car>
    <car name='Royale' make='Bugatti' year='1931'>
        <country>France</country>
        <record type='price'>Most Valuable Car at $15 million</
record>
    </car>
</records>
```

8. Download the groovy script file from `http://bit.ly/1DORckr` to any location of your choosing. Alternatively, you can get it from the code sample bundle accompanying the book.

9. Add **JSR223 PostProcessor** as a child of the Dummy Sampler by navigating to **jp@gc - Dummy Sampler | Add | Post Processors | JSR223 PostProcessor**.

10. Select **groovy** as the language of choice in the **Language** drop-down box.

11. In the **File Name** text box, put in the absolute path to where the groovy script file is, for example, `/tmp/scripts/ch7/ch7_jsr223.groovy`.

12. Add **View Results Tree** listener to **Test Plan** by navigating to **Test Plan | Add | Listener | View Results Tree**.

13. Add **Debug Sampler** to **Thread Group** by navigating to **Thread Group | Add | Sampler | Debug Sampler**.

14. Save and run the test.

15. Observe the **Response Data** tab of **Debug Sampler** and see we now have JMeter variables `car_0`, `car_1`, and `car_2`, all extracted from the response and populated by our **JSR223 PostProcessor** component.

How it works...

JMeter exposes certain variables to the JSR223 component, allowing it to get hold of sample details and information, perform logic operations, and store the results as JMeter variables. The exposed attributes include **Log**, **Label**, **Filename**, **Parameters**, **args[]**, **ctx**, **vars**, **props**, **prev**, **sampler**, and **OUT**. Each of these parameters allow access to important and useful information that can be used during the postprocessing of sampler responses.

The **Log** attribute gives access to Logger, which can be used to write log statements to the log file. The **Label** and **Filename** attribute give access to the sample label and script file name respectively. The **Parameters** and **args[]** attribute give access to parameters sent to the script. The **ctx** gives access to the current thread's JMeter context (`http://bit.ly/1lM31MC`). **vars** gives access to write values into JMeter variables (`http://bit.ly/1o5DDBr`), exposing them to the result of the test plan. The **props** attribute gives us access to JMeterProperties. The **sampler** attribute gives us access to the current sampler, while **OUT** allows us to write log statements to the standard output, that is, `System.out`. Finally, the **prev** sample gives access to the previous SampleResult (`http://bit.ly/1rKn8Cs`), allowing us to get useful information such as the response data, headers, assertion results, and so on.

In our script, we made use of the **prev** and **vars** attributes. With **prev**, we were able to get hold of the XML response from the sample. Using groovy's XmlSlurper (`http://bit.ly/1AoRMnb`), we were able to effortlessly process the XML response and compose the bits of information, and store them as JMeter variables using the **vars** attribute.

Using this technique, we are able to accomplish tasks that might have otherwise been cumbersome using any other postprocessor elements we have seen in other recipes. We are able to take full advantage of the language features of any chosen scripting language. In our case, we used groovy, but any other supported scripting languages you are comfortable with will do as well.

See also

- `http://jmeter.apache.org/usermanual/component_reference.html#BSF_PostProcessor`
- `http://jmeter.apache.org/api/org/apache/jmeter/threads/JMeterContext.html`
- `http://jmeter.apache.org/api/org/apache/jmeter/threads/JMeterVariables.html`
- `http://jmeter.apache.org/api/org/apache/jmeter/samplers/SampleResult.html`

Writing Test scripts through Ruby DSL

Sometimes, it is helpful to manually write your scripts instead of recording them. Cases such as integrating your test plans with a continuous integration build server, or being able to debug your test plans from the comfort of an **Integrated Development Environment** (**IDE**) benefit mostly from this.

Thankfully, there is a Ruby gem that provides a readable and concise DSL, allowing you to write test plans using the Ruby programming language.

How to do it...

In this recipe, we will go over how to do just that. Perform the following steps:

1. Install Ruby on your system by following the instructions given in *Appendix, Installing Supporting Software Needed for the Book*.

2. Install the JMeter DSL Ruby gem by running the following on the command prompt:

   ❏ For Mac OS:

   ```
   sudo gem install ruby-jmeter
   ```

   ❏ For Windows:

   ```
   gem install ruby-jmeter
   ```

3. On successful gem installation, you will see lines similar to the following code:

   ```
   Fetching: mime-types-2.1.gem (100%)
   Successfully installed mime-types-2.1
   Fetching: rest-client-1.6.7.gem (100%)
   Successfully installed rest-client-1.6.7
   Fetching: ruby-jmeter-2.11.2.gem (100%)
   Successfully installed ruby-jmeter-2.11.2
   Fetching: mini_portile-0.5.2.gem (100%)
   Successfully installed mini_portile-0.5.2
   Parsing documentation for mime-types-2.1
   Installing ri documentation for mime-types-2.1
   Parsing documentation for rest-client-1.6.7
   Installing ri documentation for rest-client-1.6.7
   Parsing documentation for ruby-jmeter-2.11.2
   Installing ri documentation for ruby-jmeter-2.11.2
   Parsing documentation for mini_portile-0.5.2
   Installing ri documentation for mini_portile-0.5.2
   4 gems installed
   ```

4. Open a test editor such as Notepad, Sublime, vi, Emacs, and so on.

5. Create a file named `ruby_dsl_simulation.rb` with the following content:

```ruby
require 'rubygems'
require 'ruby-jmeter'
test do
  cookies clear_each_iteration: false
  csv_data_set_config :filename => 'shoutbox-registration.txt'
  threads :count => 1 , :rampup => 1, :loops => 2 do
    defaults :domain => 'evening-citadel-2263.herokuapp.com'
    random_timer 1000, 2000
    transaction '01_shoutbox_home' do
      visit :name => 'Home', :url => '/' do
      end
    end
    transaction '02_shoutbox_signin' do
        submit :name => 'Login', :url => '/login',
        :fill_in => {
          :'user[name]' => '${user}',
          :'user[pass]' => '${pass}'
        } do
          visit :name => "home_redirect", :url => '/' do
            assert 'contains' => '${user}'
            assert 'contains' => 'logout'
          end
      end
    end
    transaction '03_logout' do
      visit :name => 'Logout', :url => '/logout' do
      end
      visit :name => 'home_redirect', :url => '/' do
        assert 'contains' => 'register'
      end
    end
  end
  view_results_tree
end.jmx(file: './ch8_ruby_dsl_simulation.jmx')
```

6. Save the file.

7. On the command line, run the following command:

    `ruby ruby_dsl_simulation.rb`

8. Open the generated test plan (`ch8_ruby_dsl_simulation.jmx`) in JMeter GUI and run it.

How it works...

The JMeter DSL gem allows you to express test plans in a clear and concise DSL, written in Ruby. The first two lines will require you to import the necessary extensions into your Ruby script in order to provide additional instructions via the DSL.

Each test block corresponds to a test plan definition in JMeter world. The cookies method defines `HttpCookieManager` to help store a user session after successful login. The `csv_data_set_config` method defines a CSV Data Set Config that we use to read our input data for the script. The threads method defines the number of threads that will run in the test plan. Optionally, you could specify how long the threads could loop for. We have defined the `HttpRequestDefaults` component using the `defaults` method, providing a base URL for our test script. Using the `transaction` method, we have grouped a series of requests into transaction controllers, similar to what we do when we record scripts manually. Finally, we use the `submit` method to log in into our application and assert successful logging in and logging out with the `ResponseAssertion` component. The `visit` method specifies the URL to go to and a friendly URL name. The `end.jmx(file: ...)` specifies the name of the file to save the test plan under when we run `ruby_dsl_simulation.rb`. It is saved as `jmeter.jmx` by default.

There's more...

The JMeter ruby gem can do a lot more than we have space to cover here. Some of the tasks, JMeter Ruby gem can perform are as follows:

- ▸ Run directly from the command line without needing to launch JMeter GUI.
- ▸ Run our script directly in the Cloud on `http://flood.io` (one of the Cloud providers offering Cloud distributed testing). See details of this in *Chapter 5, Diving into Distributed Testing*.
- ▸ Submit forms, parse responses, and more.
- ▸ Code within an IDE with code completion.

Understanding JMeter properties

In rare cases, you may need to tweak JMeter configuration to specify custom settings to use to start and run JMeter. Settings such as the default language to start JMeter GUI with, which XML parser to use, what elements to display on the GUI menu, the look and feel, the SSL settings, defining remote hosts when doing distributed testing with a master/slave setup, logging threshold, and much more can be configured using JMeter properties.

In previous versions of JMeter, all properties were defined under the `$JMETER_HOME/bin/jmeter.properties` file. This was monolithic and became a bit cumbersome to manage. Therefore, in later versions, the JMeter team has separated out these properties into additional files, `user.properties` and `system.properties`, making them a lot more concise and easier to manage. The `user.properties` file can be used to provide additional properties to configure JMeter and is considered the preferred place to define user custom settings such as classpath configuration, logging settings, and so on. This helps isolate your changes from the factory settings defined out of the box. The `system.properties` is used to update system properties such as SSL settings, keytool file location, and so on.

How to do it...

In this recipe, we will use JMeter properties to change the default language of the JMeter GUI to French, the default excludes in the script recorder, and the summarizer interval when running in non-GUI mode. Perform the following steps:

1. Open `$JMETER_HOME/bin/jmeter.properties` in any editor of your choice.

2. At the bottom of the file, enter the following property:

   ❑ **language**: `fr`

3. Save the file.

4. Launch JMeter in GUI mode.

5. Observe that all elements in the GUI are now in French.

6. Open `$JMETER_HOME/bin/jmeter.properties` and remove the language property to return to the default mode.

7. Add these two additional properties:

   ❑ **proxy.excludes.suggested**: `.*\\.(css|js)`

   ❑ **summariser.interval**: `10`

8. Save the file and launch JMeter GUI.

9. Add **HTTP(S) Test Script Recorder** to **Test Plan** by navigating to **WorkBench | Add | Non-Test Elements | HTTP(S) Test Script Recorder**.

10. Click on the **Add suggested Excludes** button.

11. Verify it `*\\.(css|js)` as we have specified.

12. Close JMeter GUI.

13. Execute a test in non-GUI mode. From the `$JMETER_HOME/bin` directory, run the following command:

    ```
    ./jmeter -n -t [absolute path to jmx file to run]
    ```

    ```
    e.g.
    ```

    ```
    ./jmeter -n -t ~/workspace/packtpub/cookbook-bundled-code/scripts/
    ch8/ch8_continuous_integration.jmx
    ```

14. Observe, the summarizer now logs the output every 10 seconds as we have defined.

How it works...

JMeter properties provide a way to alter the behavior of most aspects of JMeter. The three property files (`jmeter.properties`, `user.properties`, and `system.properties`) needed to do this to reside in the `$JMETER_HOME/bin` directory. In our recipe, we altered the language used to start the JMeter GUI in French by specifying the `language=fr` property. We then changed the default exclude lists of the HTTPS script recorder to exclude only CSS and JS (JavaScript) files by specifying the `proxy.excludes.suggested=.*\\.(css|js)` property. Finally, we changed the frequency of the summarizer logs from 30 seconds to 10 seconds by specifying `summariser.interval=10`.

There is a lot more that can be done with the `properties` file. Each `properties` file is heavily commented to give you a good grasp of what it does and how to set it. Readers are strongly encouraged to open the files and read through the comments. That is the best way to understand what options are available for you to tweak.

 A `user.properties` file can be placed in the directory where JMeter starts, which will take precedence over `user.properties` located in the `$JMETER_HOME/bin` directory.

See also

▶ The *Testing with different bandwidth* recipe

▶ Configuring JMeter (`http://jmeter.apache.org/usermanual/get-started.html#configuring_jmeter`)

Monitoring servers while executing tests (using VisualVM)

When executing test scripts, it is important to monitor the server resources where the tested application is being hosted. Resources such as CPU, memory, thread count and thread pool, I/O resources, and so on are integral to the performance of an application. Monitoring these resources helps give crucial insights into where the bottlenecks lie in the tested application or hosted environment.

How to do it...

In this recipe, we will show you how to monitor application resources using VisualVM, a tool that comes bundled with standard JDK installation files. Perform the following steps:

1. Install Maven, Git, and JDK 7 as described in the *Appendix*.

     The examples have been tested with JDK 7 only. At the time of writing this, they haven't been updated to work with JDK 8.

2. Create a directory to keep the sample code. We will refer to this as CODE_SAMPLES.
3. Open a terminal or DOS prompt and change the CODE_SAMPLES directory.
4. Clone the application using the following command:

    ```
    git clone https://github.com/jmeter-cookbook/spring-petclinic.git
    ```

5. Run the application using the following command:

    ```
    mvn tomcat7:run
    ```

     If the application started correctly, you should see a log similar to this on the console and be able to access the application at http://localhost:9966/petclinic.

```
    . . .
    INFO  RequestMappingHandlerMapping - Mapped "{[/owners/*/pets/
{petId}/visits],methods=[GET],params=[],headers=[],consumes=[]
,produces=[],custom=[]}" onto public org.springframework.web.
servlet.ModelAndView org.springframework.samples.petclinic.web.
VisitController.showVisits(int)
    INFO  SimpleUrlHandlerMapping - Mapped URL path [/resources/**]
onto handler 'org.springframework.web.servlet.resource.
ResourceHttpRequestHandler#0'
    INFO  SimpleUrlHandlerMapping - Mapped URL path [/webjars/**]
onto handler 'org.springframework.web.servlet.resource.
ResourceHttpRequestHandler#1'
    INFO  SimpleUrlHandlerMapping - Root mapping to handler
of type [class org.springframework.web.servlet.mvc.
ParameterizableViewController]
    INFO  SimpleUrlHandlerMapping - Mapped URL path [/**]
onto handler 'org.springframework.web.servlet.resource.
DefaultServletHttpRequestHandler#0'
    INFO  DispatcherServlet - FrameworkServlet 'petclinic':
initialization completed in 985 ms
    Mar 18, 2014 9:39:13 AM org.apache.coyote.AbstractProtocol start
    INFO: Starting ProtocolHandler ["http-bio-9966"]
```

6. Launch VisualVM and then perform the following steps:

    1. Go to the `bin` directory of your JDK home installation.

    2. Double-click on `jvisualvm` (or launch it from the command line).

7. Connect VisualVM to the running Java process by locating it within VisualVM and double-clicking it.

8. Launch JMeter.

9. Open the `petclinic.jmx` test script in the `scripts/ch8` directory and run it.

10. Monitor the server resources (CPU, heap (memory), classes, and threads) during your test. This is shown in the following screenshot:

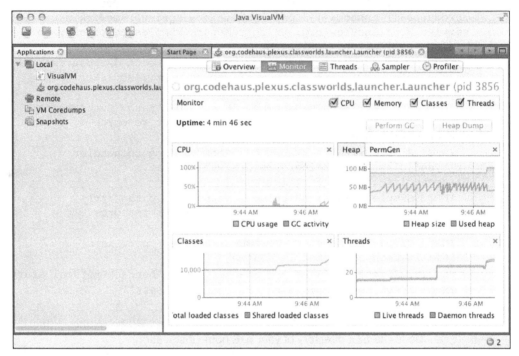

VisualVM Connecting to running application

How it works...

In step 7, when we ran `mvn tomcat7:run`, it started an embedded Apache Tomcat server and deployed an instance of our application to it. When we launched VisualVM in step 8, all the Java processes running on the system (of which our application was one) are listed and we are able to connect to it and probe it. Afterwards, JVM statistics and metrics are sent from the server to the VisualVM agent that enables it to report statistics such as heap memory usage and thread count.

There's more...

Within VisualVm, you can probe further into the application by clicking on the **Sampler** tab and clicking on the **CPU** or **Memory** tab to know what classes are taking the most CPU time or consuming the most amount of memory respectively. The **Threads** tab gives a list of all running threads in the application and their respective statuses. This can be useful to detect deadlocks and/or hangs within the application. For instance, a thread waiting for a long amount of time for a lock or resource held by another could be indicative of a race condition and defect within the application.

Finally, the **Profiler** tab allows you to gather finer-grained statistics about the running application for more detailed analysis. Within the **Profiler** tab, once the **CPU** or **Memory** button is clicked, the profiling agent attaches to the running application, and application metrics will be gathered. In the terminal, on the server console, you should see a log similar to this:

```
...
    Profiler Agent: JNI OnLoad Initializing...
    Profiler Agent: JNI OnLoad Initialized successfully
    Profiler Agent: Waiting for connection on port 5140 (Protocol
version: 12)
    Profiler Agent: Established connection with the tool
    Profiler Agent: Local accelerated session
    Profiler Agent: 250 classes cached.
...
```

The usages of profilers go way beyond the scope of this book, but we encourage you to dive deeper and understand it. It will help get you make better sense of your testing results.

VisualVM is not the only way to get such metrics. For alternatives and even more detailed profiling, please refer to the following recipes:

▸ The *Monitoring servers while executing tests (using YourKit Profiler)* recipe

▸ The *Monitoring servers while executing tests (using New Relic)* recipe

Monitoring servers while executing tests (using YourKit Profiler)

When it comes to monitoring application and machine resources, there is no shortage of available tools to aid such regard. There are a vast number of commercial tools that do a great job of this. One of such tools is YourKit Profiler.

How to do it...

In this recipe, we show you how you can monitor your server and application resources using the YourKit Profiler.

1. Install Maven, Git, and JDK 7 as described in the *Appendix*.

 The examples have been tested with JDK 7 only. At the time of writing, they haven't been updated to work with JDK 8.

2. Get a trial copy of YourKit Java Profiler from `http://yourkit.com/` and install it.

3. Create a directory to keep the sample code. We will refer to this as `CODE_SAMPLES`.

4. Open a terminal or DOS prompt and change the `CODE_SAMPLES` directory.

5. Clone the application using the following command:

   git clone https://github.com/jmeter-cookbook/spring-petclinic.git.

6. Run the application using the following command:

   mvn tomcat7:run:

 If the application started correctly, you should see a log similar to this on the console and be able to access the application at `http://localhost:9966/petclinic`. Refer the following code snippet for more information:

```
    . . .
    INFO  RequestMappingHandlerMapping - Mapped "{[/owners/*/pets/
{petId}/visits],methods=[GET],params=[],headers=[],consumes=[]
,produces=[],custom=[]}" onto public org.springframework.web.
servlet.ModelAndView org.springframework.samples.petclinic.web.
VisitController.showVisits(int)
    INFO  SimpleUrlHandlerMapping - Mapped URL path [/resources/**]
onto handler 'org.springframework.web.servlet.resource.
ResourceHttpRequestHandler#0'
    INFO  SimpleUrlHandlerMapping - Mapped URL path [/webjars/**]
onto handler 'org.springframework.web.servlet.resource.
ResourceHttpRequestHandler#1'
    INFO  SimpleUrlHandlerMapping - Root mapping to handler
of type [class org.springframework.web.servlet.mvc.
ParameterizableViewController]
    INFO  SimpleUrlHandlerMapping - Mapped URL path [/**]
onto handler 'org.springframework.web.servlet.resource.
DefaultServletHttpRequestHandler#0'
    INFO  DispatcherServlet - FrameworkServlet 'petclinic':
initialization completed in 985 ms
    Mar 18, 2014 9:39:13 AM org.apache.coyote.AbstractProtocol start
    INFO: Starting ProtocolHandler ["http-bio-9966"]
```

7. Launch YourKit.

8. Connect YourKit to the running Java process by locating it within YourKit and double-clicking on it and perform the following step. On successful connection, you should see a log similar to the following one on the server console:

   ```
   [YourKit Java Profiler 2013 build 13050] Log file: /Users/
   berinle/.yjp/log/Launcher-8713.log
   ```

9. Launch JMeter.

10. Open the `petclinic.jmx` test script in the `scripts/ch8` directory and run it.

11. In YourKit, click on the **Performance Charts** tab and monitor the server resources (CPU, heap (memory), classes and threads) during your test.

12. Stop the test and view the results as shown in the following screenshot:

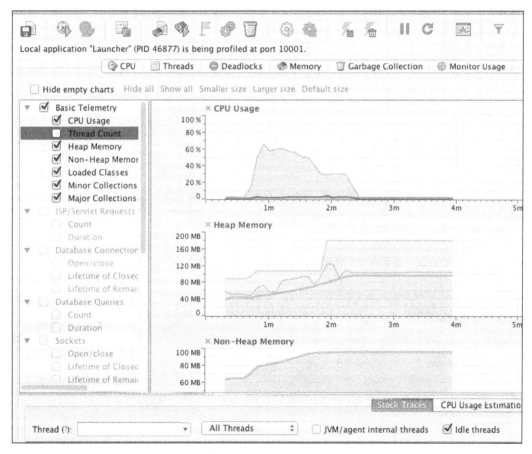

YourKit Connecting to running application

How it works...

In step 7, when we ran `mvn tomcat7:run`, the command started an embedded Apache Tomcat server and deployed an instance of our application to it. When we launched YourKit Profiler in step 9, all the Java processes running on the system (of which our application was one) were listed and we were able to connect to it and probe it. Afterwards, JVM statistics and metrics were sent from the server to the YourKit agent, which enabled it to report statistics such as CPU usage, heap memory usage, and thread count to name a few.

There's more...

YourKit is a full pledged Java profiler that gives you a detailed analysis of the various aspects of an application. You can introspect the memory and look further into which objects are taking too much memory on the heap, which methods are causing the application to drag, potential memory leaks in an application, and so on. Other profilers are available and they all give about the same insight into an application's inner workings.

Other popular known profilers include JProfiler and JProbe.

Detailing all the workings of a profiler go beyond this book. Curious readers are encouraged to find out more profilers by doing a web search and/or reading the help documentation that comes with the profiler. For YourKit Profiler discussed in this section, details can be found on their site at `http://yourkit.com/`.

YourKit is not the only way to get such metrics but it is definitely better at doing the job, being a full pledged profiler. For alternatives, please refer to the following recipes:

 ▸ The *Monitoring Servers while executing tests (using VisualVM)* recipe
 ▸ The *Monitoring Servers while executing tests (using New Relic)* recipe

Monitoring servers while executing tests (using New Relic)

When you are profiling an application that is deployed in the Cloud, using any of the other discussed profiling methods cannot work. In such cases, if the Cloud provider offers integration with New Relic (which most do), then you can profile the application using the method described here.

New Relic (`http://www.newrelic.com`) is an application performance management and monitoring tool. It allows you connect to your applications running on Cloud servers and get performance metrics and insights like you would get when running locally. It's a commercial tool, but they do offer a free account that is sufficient for us to illustrate the concepts in this recipe.

How to do it...

In this recipe, we will show you can monitor your server and application resources using New Relic. Perform the following steps:

1. Install Maven, Git, and JDK 7 as described in the *Appendix*.

 The examples have been tested with JDK 7 only. At the time of writing, they haven't been updated to work with JDK 8.

Sign up for a free Heroku account at `http://www.heroku.com`.

1. Install Heroku toolbelt for your operating system as described at `https://toolbelt.heroku.com/`.

2. Create a directory to keep the sample code. We will refer to this as CODE_SAMPLES.

3. Open a terminal or DOS prompt and change the CODE_SAMPLES directory.

4. Clone the application using the following command:

    `git clone https://github.com/jmeter-cookbook/spring-petclinic.git`

5. Deploy the application on Heroku and run the following command:

    `heroku create`

    1. If this is successful, you should see the following log (yours will be different as Heroku assigns random names to newly created applications.):

        ```
        Creating frozen-headland-2987... done, stack is cedar
        http://frozen-headland-2987.herokuapp.com/ | git@heroku.
        com:frozen-headland-2987.git
            Git remote heroku added
        ```

    2. Run the following command:

        `git push heroku master`

3. If all checks out, you should see logs similar to the following:

```
Initializing repository, done.
Counting objects: 3632, done.
Delta compression using up to 8 threads.
Compressing objects: 100% (1988/1988), done.
Writing objects: 100% (3632/3632), 847.01 KiB | 0 bytes/s,
done.
Total 3632 (delta 1127), reused 3615 (delta 1113)
-----> Java app detected
-----> Installing OpenJDK ... done
-----> Installing Maven 3.0.3... done
-----> Installing settings.xml... done
-----> executing /app/tmp/cache/.maven/bin/mvn -B -Duser.
home=/tmp/build_85518f88-fc2e-4468-b487-80acd6cff8bb
-Dmaven.repo.local=/app/tmp/cache/.m2/repository -s /app/
tmp/cache/.m2/settings.xml -DskipTests=true clean install
        [INFO] Scanning for projects...
        [INFO]
        [INFO] -------------------------------------------
----------------------------
        [INFO] Building petclinic 1.0.0-SNAPSHOT
        [INFO] -------------------------------------------
----------------------------
        Downloading: http://s3pository.heroku.com/jvm/
org/apache/maven/plugins/maven-compiler-plugin/3.0/maven-
compiler-plugin-3.0.pom
    .........
        [INFO] -------------------------------------------
----------------------------
        [INFO] BUILD SUCCESS
        [INFO] -------------------------------------------
----------------------------
        [INFO] Total time: 51.380s
        [INFO] Finished at: Thu Mar 20 09:51:04 UTC 2014
        [INFO] Final Memory: 20M/493M
        [INFO] -------------------------------------------
----------------------------
    -----> Discovering process types
        Procfile declares types -> web
    -----> Compressing... done, 98.3MB
    -----> Launching... done, v6
        http://frozen-headland-2987.herokuapp.com/ deployed
to Heroku
```

6. Verify that the application was successfully deployed by either copying the provided URL in the browser or running the following on the command line:

```
heroku open
```

Add the New Relic add-on to your deployed application and do the following:

❏ Run the following command:

```
heroku addons:add newrelic:stark
```

❏ You should see the following logs:

```
Adding newrelic:stark on frozen-headland-2987... done, v7
(free)

Use `heroku addons:docs newrelic` to view documentation.
```

❏ Run the following command to bind a name to your application for identification on New Relic:

```
heroku config:set NEW_RELIC_APP_NAME="Spring Petclinic"
```

7. View metric results on the New Relic dashboard and perform the following steps:

1. Go to your Heroku dashboard at `https://dashboard.herokuapp.com`, and select the app for which you have installed the New Relic add-on.

2. Alternatively, you can run Heroku add-ons: open New Relic from the terminal window to go directly to the New Relic dashboard.

3. Select New Relic from your list of add-ons.

4. For more information on working with New Relic, see the New Relic documentation at `https://newrelic.com/docs/`.

 It could take up to 5 minutes before your application metrics are reported to the New Relic dashboard.

8. Open the `petclinic-heroku.jmx` file in the `scripts/ch8` directory.

9. Click on **User Defined Variables** and change the `base_url` to match the URL of your assigned application, that is, `<your-app-name>.herokuapp.com`.

10. Save your changes and run the test.

11. Monitor the server and application resources in the New Relic dashboard.

12. Stop the test and view the results as shown in the following screenshot:

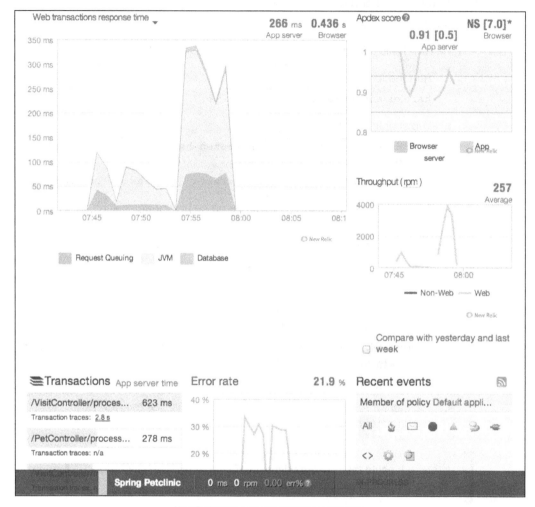

New Relic connecting to running application

 We renamed our deployed application on Heroku afterwards and the actual sample deployed at the time of writing is now available at `http://petclinic-jcb.herokuapp.com/`.

How it works...

In step 9, we deployed our application to Heroku's Cloud platform when we ran the Git push Heroku master application. This in turn stated an embedded Jetty server and deployed our application to it. In step 10, we verified that the application was successfully deployed by making sure it was accessible by running Heroku. We then added the New Relic monitoring capabilities to our application when we ran Heroku add-ons: docs, and newrelic: stark in step 11. Once added, our application was restarted on Heroku and within 5 minutes, the application and server metrics were sent to the New Relic monitoring dashboard. New Relic gives numerous metrics for our application including CPU and memory usage, top requests, throughput, database monitoring (seeing top queries from within our application), and so on.

 Some of the features such as database monitoring are not part of the free tier. However, New Relic allows you upgrade your account to a pro account from a trial once the add-on is added.

There's more...

New Relic works with a variety of technology stacks including Java (which we illustrated in this recipe), Node.js, and Rails, to name a few. When testing applications deployed in the Cloud, it is a handy and valuable tool to introspect application performance and resource consumption.

More details can be found on New Relic's site at http://www.newrelic.com.

See also

For alternatives, please refer to the following recipes:

▶ The *Monitoring servers while executing tests (using VisualVM)* recipe

▶ The *Monitoring servers while executing tests (using YourKit Profiler)* recipe

▶ The PerfMon plugin for JMeter
(http://jmeter-plugins.org/wiki/PerfMon/)

Performance tips to scale JMeter

When you need to simulate a large load in test runs—for instance, more than a couple of hundred users—it is important to follow certain measures to ensure you get the best out of JMeter. Though there is no one-size-fits-all approach to determine how much load can be put on a certain machine, as this depends on the type of application, network settings, machine resources, and several other factors, we can still adhere to certain guidelines to get the most out of JMeter regardless of the nature of your tests or applications under test.

How to do it...

In this recipe, we will point out some guidelines that will help you get more performance out of JMeter. Perform the following steps:

1. You need to know the approximate capacity/load for machine(s) which use to perform your tests can handle for a given application under tests:

    ❑   A machine with 4GB RAM and a quad-core 2.4 GHz processor, running JMeter with 1GB of heap, can usually run 200-250 users before starting to deteriorate in performance. Also, a test plan with delays between requests, will be able to handle larger loads than those without, as the machine's resources are not as stressed as in the latter case.

2. Favor multiple slave nodes with no master configuration over master/slave setup.

    ❑   When scaling out JMeter, that is, running in distributed mode, you are better off running separate instances of JMeter per node machine than running in a master/slave configuration.

    ❑   Though there are some benefits to running distributed tests as a master/slave configuration (for example, a consolidated place to control slave machines, aggregated reporting, and so on), the overhead quickly outweighs the benefits when you have more than a couple of slave machines. The master node is overwhelmed and becomes the bottleneck.

3. Run in non-GUI mode.

    ❑   The GUI mode is fine for recording, building, and running preliminary tests, but it is not recommended to use for large scale testing since it in itself consumes some resources. For large scale testing, the command line is your friend. You can spin off tests from the command line using the following command:

    ```
    jmeter[.bat] -n -t [absolute path to test file]
    ```

    From the $JMETR_HOME/bin directory:

    ❑   On Windows:

    ```
    jmeter.bat -n -t c:\jmeter-test-plan.jmx
    ```

    ❑   On Unix:

    ```
    ./jmeter -n -t /tmp/jmeter-test-plan.jmx
    ```

4. Disable all listeners in your test plans.

   ❏ While listeners are beneficial for preliminary testing, they can have adverse effects on performance. Some listeners consume more resources than others. Listeners such as View Results Tree and graph plotting listeners are known suspects for high resource consumption. Instead, you can run in non-GUI mode specifying a results JTL file and use the JTL file view with the results of your test after it has completed, using any listener component such as the Aggregate Report listener. All JMeter listener components have a file input box where you can select existing results files to view at any time. An example of specifying a log file is as follows:

   ```
   ./jmeter -n -t ~/workspace/packtpub/cookbook-bundled-code/
   scripts/ch8/ch8_mobile_website.jmx -l /tmp/mobile.jtl
   ```

5. Use timers in your scripts.

   ❏ Ideally, your tests are meant to simulate realistic behaviors and conditions. For example, when browsing a web application, a user would normally pause for a duration of time between page clicks and requests. By default, pauses are not captured when you record test scripts. Be sure you put some pauses in test plans.

6. Understand the application requirements and the test target goals.

   ❏ When developing test plans, it is crucial to understand the requirements of the application under test so as to develop relevant, useful, and comprehensive test plans that meet their criteria.

7. Performance testing and tuning are best friends.

   ❏ The goal of performance testing is often to ensure the application under test meets certain criteria set by stakeholders. Under heavy load, the application will exhibit some errors or slowness that might not have been seen under low or moderate load. The errors or slowness could be due to some application component or system configuration that needs to be tweaked. This often leads to a series of tune-test cycle to identify, isolate, and hopefully resolve the bottleneck.

 As a rule of thumb, make only one change at a time to know whether the change had a positive or negative impact on performance.

8. Keep a profiler and monitoring tools close at hand.

   ❑ Without adequate tools to monitor the system, network, and application metrics, exercising performance test is like shooting in the dark. You will almost certainly fail to hit your target. As such, it is important you have insight into all the layers involved in your testing to pinpoint exactly the root causes of issues when they arise. This is often not a simple task, but having the right tools certainly gets you a step closer.

How it works...

We have highlighted some common guidelines we have learned and followed over the years as we aim to get the best performance out of JMeter when scaling it. It is important to know the limitation of your test machines and plan accordingly. A master/slave setup can't be used for any serious load testing spanning for more than a couple of machines. A better approach is to avoid a master altogether and accumulate results from node machines post-test. Disabling listeners, using timers, and running in non-GUI mode saves resources and enables you put more load on a test server. It is also crucial to have insights into all the layers of the application under test, including the system, network, metrics, and so on, to adequately diagnose and resolve issues encountered.

This is by no means an exhaustive list, but these are good starter guidelines as you prepare to scale JMeter.

See also

- The *Using timers* recipe in *Chapter 1, JMeter Fundamentals*
- The *Testing external facing applications using Flood.IO* recipe in *Chapter 5, Diving into Distributed Testing*
- The *Testing external facing applications using BlazeMeter* recipe in *Chapter 5, Diving into Distributed Testing*
- The *Using Throughput Shaping Timer* recipe in *Chapter 6, Extending JMeter*
- The *Using Constant Throughput Timer* recipe in *Chapter 7, Building, Debugging, and Analyzing the Results of Test Plans*
- http://blazemeter.com/blog/5-ways-launch-jmeter-test-without-using-jmeter-gui
- http://blazemeter.com/blog/how-reduce-memory-usage-jmeter

Installing the Supporting Software Needed for this Book

In this appendix, we will cover the following recipes:

- ▶ Installing JMeter
- ▶ Installing Java Development Kit (JDK)
- ▶ Installing JMeter plugins
- ▶ Installing Vagrant
- ▶ Installing VirtualBox
- ▶ Installing Maven
- ▶ Installing Git
- ▶ Obtaining AWS keys for EC2

Introduction

During the course of the book, we have installed several types of supporting software needed to follow along with some of the recipes. At such times, we have asked you to refer to the appendix for installation instructions.

In this appendix, we'll cover how to install the needed software to successfully follow along with those recipes.

Installing JMeter

Perform the following steps to install JMeter on your system:

1. Navigate to `http://jmeter.apache.org/download_jmeter.cgi`.
2. Download version 2.11 by clicking on the ZIP or gz archive under the **Binaries** section.
3. If you don't find this version there, you can download it from the older archives page at `http://archive.apache.org/dist/jmeter/binaries/`.
4. Extract the archive to the location of your chosen directory.

We refer to this location as `JMETER_HOME` throughout the book.

One line install

Assuming you have `curl` installed on your system, then you can do the following:

For the `tar gzip` archive:

```
curl -L -O http://mirror.metrocast.net/apache//jmeter/binaries/apache-
jmeter-2.11.tgz && tar xzf apache-jmeter-2.11.tgz
```

For the ZIP archive:

```
curl -L -O http://mirror.metrocast.net/apache//jmeter/binaries/apache-
jmeter-2.11.zip && unzip apache-jmeter-2.11.zip
```

Installing Java Development Kit (JDK)

Perform the following steps to install the JDK on your system:

1. Download the latest version (Java SE 7u67 at the time of writing this book) of the Java 7 JDK (not 8) from Oracle at `http://www.oracle.com/technetwork/java/javase/downloads/index.html`.
2. Agree to the license agreements.
3. Pick the installer compatible with your system.
4. Double-click on the installer and follow the onscreen instructions.

See also

▶ `http://docs.oracle.com/javase/7/docs/webnotes/install/index.html`

Installing JMeter plugins

Perform the following steps to install JMeter plugins on your system:

1. Download the latest standard set of plugin from `http://jmeter-plugins.org/`. At the time of writing this book, it was version 1.1.3. Alternatively, you can download it directly from `http://jmeter-plugins.org/downloads/file/JMeterPlugins-Standard-1.1.3.zip`.

2. Extract the contents of the ZIP archive into the `JMETER_HOME` directory.

One line install

Assuming you have `JMETER_HOME` defined, run the following command on your console window:

```
export JMETER_HOME=/tmp/apache-jmeter-2.11
curl -L -O http://jmeter-plugins.org/downloads/file/JMeterPlugins-Standard-1.1.3.zip  && unzip -o JMeterPlugins-Standard-1.1.3.zip -d $JMETER_HOME
```

See also

▶ `http://jmeter-plugins.org/wiki/PluginInstall/`

Installing Vagrant

Perform the following steps to install Vagrant on your system:

1. Download the Vagrant installer compatible with your system from `http://www.vagrantup.com/downloads.html`. At the time of writing this book, version 1.6.3 is the latest version, and that is what was used in the book.

2. Once downloaded, double-click on the installer and follow the onscreen instructions.

 If needed, the older versions of the installer can be retrieved from `http://www.vagrantup.com/downloads-archive.html`.

See also

▶ `http://www.vagrantup.com`

Installing VirtualBox

For you to be able to do anything with Vagrant, you need to have VirtualBox or VMFusion. VirtualBox is freely available while VMFusion is not. We have opted to use VirtualBox in the book for this reason alone, so everyone can follow along without needing to pay for commercial ware. Perform the following steps:

1. Download a VirtualBox installer compatible with your system from `https://www.virtualbox.org/wiki/Downloads`. At the time of writing this book, version 4.3.14 is the latest version, and that is what was used in the book.

2. Once downloaded, double-click on the installer and follow the onscreen instructions.

 If needed, the older versions of the installer can be retrieved from `https://www.virtualbox.org/wiki/Download_Old_Builds`.

See also

▶ `https://www.virtualbox.org`

Installing Maven

Perform the following steps to install Maven on your system:

1. Download Maven from `http://maven.apache.org/download.cgi`. At the time of writing this book, version 3.2.3 is the latest version, and that is what was used in the book.

2. Once downloaded, extract the archive to the location of your chosen directory. We refer to this as `M2_HOME`.

3. Include the extracted location in your path variable so that `mvn` is available on the terminal:

   ❑ For example, if you extracted the archive to `c:\devtools\apache-maven-3.2.3` on Windows, or `/Users/bayo/devtools/apache-maven-3.2.3` on Unix/Mac OS, you will proceed with the following steps:

   ❑ On Windows:
   ```
   set M2_HOME=c:\devtools\apache-maven-3.2.3
   set PATH=%PATH%;%M2_HOME%\bin;
   ```

❑ On Unix/Mac OS:

```
export M2_HOME=/Users/bayo/devtools/apache-maven-3.2.3
export PATH=$PATH:$M2_HOME/bin
```

Alternatively, you could set these in your shell profiles, for example, `~/.zshrc` (for Zsh) or `~/.bash_profile` (for Bash) for convenience.

Installing Git

Perform the following steps to install Git on your system:

1. Download Git from `http://git-scm.com/downloads`.
2. Once downloaded, double-click on the installer and follow the onscreen instructions.

Obtaining AWS keys for EC2

To obtain AWS access keys, which are needed for recipes in *Chapter 5*, *Diving into Distributed Testing*, perform the following steps:

1. Create a free AWS account if you don't already have one by navigating to `http://aws.amazon.com/` and clicking on the **Sign up** or **Create a Free Account** button.
2. Once your account has been created, go to the IAM console at `https://console.aws.amazon.com/iam/home?#home`.
3. Click on the **Users** link on the sidebar.
4. Select your IAM username and select **User Actions | Manage Access Keys**:
   - ❑ Create a new user by clicking on the **Create New Users** button and following the onscreen instructions
   - ❑ Note the Access Key ID and Secret Access Key of the newly created user and download them
5. Click on the **Create Access Key** button:
   - ❑ A new key/secret pair is generated and can be downloaded
6. Click on the **Download** credentials.

See also

▶ `http://docs.aws.amazon.com/AWSSimpleQueueService/latest/SQSGettingStartedGuide/AWSCredentials.html`

Index

F

file downloads
dealing with 42, 43
files
uploading, with scripts 58, 59
File Transfer Protocol (FTP) 90
Firefox
Firepath Plugin 46
Flood.IO
URL 118, 173
used, for testing external
facing applications 118-121
ForEach Controller
about 72
leveraging, in test plans 69-72
URL 69
FoxyProxy
about 14
URL 14
FTP services
testing 90-94

G

Git
download link 205
installing 205
Google Chrome
download link 17
XPath Helper 46
Gradle
URL 143
graphical user interface (GUI) 94
Groovy
URL 156
groovy-all JAR file
download link 138
Groovy script file
download link 157
Groovy Server Pages (GSP) 31

H

H2 database
download link 95
setting up 95
Har2jmeter 22

Heroku
toolbelt, installing 193
URL 193
URL, for dashboard 195
HTML responses
handling 50-53
HTTP Cache Manager component
using 176
working 177
HTTP Header Properties 129
HTTP(S) Test Script Recorder
about 16
used, for recording script 12-14
HTTP user sessions
managing 27, 28
HTTP web archives (HAR)
converting, to JMeter test plans 19-22

I

installation
Git 205
Java Development Kit (JDK) 202
JMeter 202
JMeter plugins 203
Maven 204
Vagrant 203
VirtualBox 204
**Integrated Development
Environment (IDE) 181**
Interleave Controller
about 77
using, in test plans 72-76
internal applications
testing, JMeter used 109-112
testing, Vagrant used 109-112

J

Java Archives (JARs) 125
Java Message Service. *See* **JMS services**
Java Runtime Environment (JRE) 96
Java Server Pages (JSP) 31
Java Virtual Machine (JVM) 143
Java Development Kit (JDK)
download link 202
installing 202

Thank you for buying
JMeter Cookbook

About Packt Publishing

Packt, pronounced 'packed', published its first book "*Mastering phpMyAdmin for Effective MySQL Management*" in April 2004 and subsequently continued to specialize in publishing highly focused books on specific technologies and solutions.

Our books and publications share the experiences of your fellow IT professionals in adapting and customizing today's systems, applications, and frameworks. Our solution based books give you the knowledge and power to customize the software and technologies you're using to get the job done. Packt books are more specific and less general than the IT books you have seen in the past. Our unique business model allows us to bring you more focused information, giving you more of what you need to know, and less of what you don't.

Packt is a modern, yet unique publishing company, which focuses on producing quality, cutting-edge books for communities of developers, administrators, and newbies alike. For more information, please visit our website: www.packtpub.com.

About Packt Open Source

In 2010, Packt launched two new brands, Packt Open Source and Packt Enterprise, in order to continue its focus on specialization. This book is part of the Packt Open Source brand, home to books published on software built around Open Source licenses, and offering information to anybody from advanced developers to budding web designers. The Open Source brand also runs Packt's Open Source Royalty Scheme, by which Packt gives a royalty to each Open Source project about whose software a book is sold.

Writing for Packt

We welcome all inquiries from people who are interested in authoring. Book proposals should be sent to author@packtpub.com. If your book idea is still at an early stage and you would like to discuss it first before writing a formal book proposal, contact us; one of our commissioning editors will get in touch with you.

We're not just looking for published authors; if you have strong technical skills but no writing experience, our experienced editors can help you develop a writing career, or simply get some additional reward for your expertise.

Performance Testing with JMeter 2.9

ISBN: 978-1-78216-584-2   Paperback: 148 pages

Learn how to test web applications using Apache JMeter with practical, hands-on examples

1. Create realistic and maintainable scripts for web applications.

2. Use various JMeter components to achieve testing goals.

3. Removal of unnecessary errors and code compilation.

4. Acquire skills that will enable you to leverage the Cloud for distributed testing.

Metasploit Penetration Testing Cookbook

Second Edition

ISBN: 978-1-78216-678-8   Paperback: 320 pages

Over 80 recipes to master the most widely used penetration testing framework

1. Special focus on the latest operating systems, exploits, and penetration testing techniques for wireless, VOIP, and Cloud.

2. This book covers a detailed analysis of third-party tools based on the Metasploit framework to enhance the penetration testing experience.

3. Detailed penetration testing techniques for different specializations like wireless networks, VOIP systems with a brief introduction to penetration testing in the Cloud.

Please check **www.PacktPub.com** for information on our titles

Mapping and Visualization with SuperCollider

ISBN: 978-1-78328-967-7   Paperback: 222 pages

Create interactive and responsive audio-visual applications with SuperCollider

1. Master 2D computer-generated graphics and animation.

2. Perform complex encodings and audio/data analysis.

3. Implement intelligent generative audio-visual systems.

Application Testing with Capybara

ISBN: 978-1-78328-125-1   Paperback: 104 pages

Confidently implement automated tests for web applications using Capybara

1. Learn everything to become super productive with this highly acclaimed test automation library.

2. Using some advanced features, turn yourself into a Capybara ninja!

3. Packed with practical examples and easy-to-follow sample mark-up and test code.

Please check **www.PacktPub.com** for information on our titles

www.ingramcontent.com/pod-product-compliance
Lightning Source LLC
Chambersburg PA
CBHW060551060326
40690CB00017B/3674